Telling
Training's Story

Telling Training's Story

Evaluation Made Simple, Credible, and Effective

Robert O. Brinkerhoff

BERRETT-KOEHLER PUBLISHERS, INC.
San Francisco

Berrett-Koehler Publishers, Inc.
235 Montgomery Street. Suite 650
San Francisco, CA 94104-2916
Tel: 415-288-0260 Fax: 415-362-2512 www.bkconnection.com

Ordering Information

Quantity sales Special discounts are available on quantity purchases by corporations, associations, and others. For details, contact the "Special Sales Department" at the Berrett-Koehler address above.

Individual sales Berrett-Koehler publications are available through most bookstores. They can also be ordered direct from Berrett-Koehler: Tel: (800) 929-2929; Fax (802) 864-7626.

Orders for college textbook/course adoption use Please contact Berrett-Koehler:
Tel: (800) 929-2929; Fax (802) 864-7626.

Orders by U.S. trade bookstores and wholesalers Please contact Ingram Publisher Services,
Tel: (800) 509-4887; Fax: (800) 838-1149; E-mail: customer.service@ingrampublisherservices.com; or visit www.ingrampublisherservices.com/Ordering for details about electronic ordering.

Berrett-Koehler and BK logo are registered trademarks of Berrett-Koehler Publishers, Inc.

Printed in the United States of America

Berrrett-Koehler books are printed on long-lasting acid-free paper. When it is available, we choose paper that has been manufactured by environmentally responsible processes. These may include using trees grown in sustainable forests, incorporating recycled paper, minimizing chlorine in bleaching, or recycling the energy produced at the paper mill.

Library of Congress Cataloging-in-Publication Data

Brinkerhoff, Robert O.
  Telling training's story: evaluation made simple, credible, and effective / Robert O. Brinkerhoff.
    p. cm.
  Includes bibliographical references and index.
  ISBN 978-1-57675-186-2
    1. Employees—Training of—Evaluation. I. Title

  HF5549.5.T7B656 2005
  658.31'12404—dc22

                                                                    2005054585

First Edition
10 09 08   10 9 8 7 6 5 4 3 2

Book Design & Production: Jimmie Young • Copy Editing: Cecile Kaufman

*To my wife, Stevie, my children, Jory, Darcy, Susanna, and Allie,
my love for whom is my beginning and my end.
I want to make a special note also to the memory of Malcolm Provus,
my dear friend and doctoral advisor, who started me on my convoluted
career path. His untimely death at the age of 46 robbed too many
of us of his inspiration and caring energy.*

Contents

Preface

Most of us in the training and development profession know in our guts that what we do is valuable and worthwhile—we wouldn't have stuck with this job if we didn't believe we were doing good. The problem is that often our clients and customers are highly skeptical, and when there is pressure on resources, we usually get the short end of the budget stick. Customers and senior executives want proof, but most of us can only offer promises.

It is clear that we need to provide credible and valid evidence of training impact and show the difference training makes to the bottom line. There have been many workshops and books and articles written about evaluation of training, and many of them offer good advice and at least partially effective methods. The problem is that too many of these methods and tools are too elaborate, too complex, too costly, take too much time, or take a Ph.D. level of knowledge to understand or use.

Using the methods and tools in this book, you can discover, measure, and document the great results that training helps your organization to achieve, and report them in a way that senior leaders find compelling and believable. You will not have to rely on sophisticated and elaborate statistical methods or suspicious assumptions and extrapolations. Instead, the Success Case Method will let you tell the story of training impact and bottom-line value with evidence that would stand up in court, making a clear and inarguable case that training indeed pays off and helps your organization be more successful, durable, and competitive.

The Success Case method (SCM) is robust enough to withstand scrutiny from a scientific and research perspective but will not choke real-world practitioners and their clients with cumbersome methods and arcane statistical gyrations. On the other hand, it is simple enough for the typical practitioner to use and will not be scoffed at by chief financial officers and others wanting to see real and credible "bottom line" evidence of training impact and value.

The Success Case Method (SCM) measures and evaluates training sensibly—accurately, simply, and quickly, and above all in a way that is both extremely credible and compelling. Better yet, the results are actionable. We have learned how we can make very strategic and constructive use of our evaluation findings, actually helping clients be more effective and successful. We can justify spending resources on evaluating training because it pays off - evaluation results themselves are worth the money we spend to get them. We can make a good return-on-investment (ROI) argument for evaluation.

There is another wonderful pay off for the method explained in this book. For decades training and development professionals have recognized that manager support for training is absolutely vital to success. When managers support training and learners, it works. When they do not, it does not. As a result, we have begged and cajoled managers to support our efforts. But inevitably, despite our pleas, most managers find other things more important to do, paying lip-service only to the grand tools and guidelines we create for them. With the Success Case Method, we are able to give them a clear and data-based business case for supporting training. We can show them specific actions they can take to reinforce learning and performance, and tie these directly to bottom-line results and economic payoff to them and to their organizations. Then, rather than trying to make all sorts of mandatory prescriptions for support actions, we can simply show managers the data and let them do what they are paid to do: look at the facts and make a business decision.

The SCM does not just measure and document the impact of training, it uncovers and pinpoints the factors that make or break training success. Then it shows how these factors can be managed more effectively so that more learning turns into worthwhile performance in the future. It is aimed directly at helping leaders in an organization discover their organization's "learning disabilities" then figure out what needs to be done to overcome these problems. Over time, the SCM helps an organization become better and better at turning an ounce of training investment into a pound of impactive performance.

The SCM approach for evaluation can be used for more good things than just pleading the case for your existence. Not that making the argument for your budget is a bad thing to do. It is certainly a good thing to be able to show your customers and bosses that what you do pays off, and that their investment of dollars in your function is worthwhile. You need this information, and they do too. But if this were all that you could do with training evaluation results you would soon, and rightfully so, encounter resistance. Diverting resources from your central mission in order to defend your budgets and pat yourself on the back for a job well done is not a good enough reason to spend more of your organization's precious resources, even if the evaluation process you use, like the Success Case Method, is relatively inexpensive.

My colleagues and I had been nibbling around the edges of this approach—the Success Case Method—for a long time. It just took us a while to figure out how to make it as strong and yet as easy to do in evaluating training programs as it has become today. It also took a lot of work with many clients and colleagues who put it to use and began to get great results with it. Companies such as Hewlett Packard, Delta Airlines, Ingersoll Rand, Daimler Chrysler, Pfizer, and Pitney Bowes (among dozens of others) have used this method and helped make it robust and practical.

I have been working at and writing about measuring training for more than 30 years. I am by profession and reputation a "world renowned" expert in evaluation and measurement. I completed a doctoral degree in program evaluation and learned a raft of sophisticated methods and techniques for partialing out causes of things, making complex statistical analyses, and conducting all sorts of tests and measurements. Yet only in the recent past ten years or so have I finally figured out how to do this evaluation work sensibly and simply. While it may have taken a long time to get here, I am proud to write this book, and prouder still of the evaluation method and tools described in these pages.

Each year, companies and organizations across the globe spend billions and billions of dollars providing training and education to their employees. The good news is that by and large this investment is worthwhile and pays off. The bad news is that it does not pay off anywhere near as much as it could and should. Worse yet, the effects of training, even when it is very successful, have been perennially hard to measure and prove. When it comes to being able to show whether a single training program is making a worthwhile difference or not, most training and development professionals are at a loss for a good answer.

In the first chapter of the book, I explain the simple and basic concept of the Success Case Method (SCM) for evaluating training, showing how we solve the riddle of measuring training impact in a way that makes it clear, specific, and believable. The second chapter presents the strategic framework for the SCM. This shows how the SCM pays for itself by creating results that an organization can use to improve management capability and performance. How the SCM works and the five steps in

planning and implementing a SCM evaluation form the content of the
third chapter. Chapter Four through Chapter Eight are each dedicated
to in-depth instructions and guidelines for carrying out each of the five
SCM steps. The closing four chapters present, one chapter per example,
case study summaries of actual SCM evaluations carried out in major
global organizations. These are authored by previous SCM clients and
professional colleagues who are dedicated SCM practitioners.

Liberal examples, illustrations, tools, checklists and guidelines are
included throughout the book. In short, the book not only tells you
about the Success Case Method for evaluating training, it shows you step
by step how to do your own SCM projects and how to help you and your
organization benefit from them.

Acknowledgements

Mal Provus got me thinking about all of this evaluation work in the first place and, through his dogged insistence, instilled in me the goal of putting evaluation tools and methods into the hands of lay practitioners. His inspiration got the ball rolling, and many have helped me since. Valerie Brown, Dennis Dressler, and Tim Fallon all played key roles in the early development of the Success Case Method (SCM). Michael Scriven's interest, trust, encouragement and deeply thoughtful intellect helped elevate and strengthen this evaluation approach and make it the practical but powerful method it is today.

My good friends and colleagues at Advantage Performance Group (APG)—leaders Glenn Jackson, John Hoskins, Tim Mooney and Alan Meeker, and the many partners who pioneered SCM projects with their clients: Peg Ruppert, Steve Gielda, Bob Thomason, Francine Smilen, Mary Steiner, Kelvin Yao, Jeff Tucker and others—helped us spread the Success Case Method gospel among APG's many thoughtful and committed clients. APG has also invested heavily in SCM training and resource development so that others can readily access SCM support and services. Richard Hodge and his other amazingly creative colleagues at the Real

Learning Company have leveraged the SCM with their many clients and helped us develop tools to support SCM users. Marguerite Foxon from Motorola has been a long-time supporter and SCM enthusiast and loyally provides us with her wit and energy to improve it. Our Northern Europe partner, Conny Bauer, not only took the time from her busy SCM practice to contribute a chapter, but likewise encourages and contributes to the improvement of our SCM services. Scott Blanchard of the Ken Blanchard Companies continues to rely on the SCM to demonstrate to his clients the worthwhile business impact his coaching and training services regularly deliver.

And last, thanks to our hundreds of clients whose opportunities to practice our craft and high expectations for credible and actionable results tempered our thinking and kept us grounded in the realities of useful work.

Part I

Chapter One

Getting to the Heart of Training Impact

*J*an Westbourne had a lot going for her—she was attractive, energetic, bright, and an MBA from the University of Massachusetts. To top it off, she drove an old 60's Porsche Speedster during the Maine summers, switching to a newer SUV for the long winter. Just two years out of her graduate program, she worked in the thriving American Express Financial Advisors office in Portland. All in all, life should have been pretty good for Jan.

But things were not going well. Jan was ranked at the bottom of the 32 fellow advisors in her office. Here she sat in last place, with low performance metrics and a productivity record that put her in the bottom ranks of advisors nationally with her tenure in the company.

It was not for lack of trying. Like others in the office, Jan made telephone "cold calls," trying to land initial appointments from the long list of prospects the office head provided. But she struggled. The lengthy list of names in front of her would swim in her vision and seem to grow interminably longer in front of her eyes. She would hear echoing voices even before the call of the rejection she was certain she would get. Sometimes, her confidence would flag so much that *she could make only one or two calls. As soon as she got a particularly nasty negative response, she'd pack up and head home, choking back the hot tears that threatened to overtake her if anyone spoke to her.*

Her failure nagged at her. This was not how she saw herself—a dean's list graduate and, in her own estimation, a financial analysis whiz. Her friends in school noted and envied her air of self confidence. If they could see her now they would change their tunes. She was fine in client meetings, and in fact could close a sale almost as well as the best in her office. Her problem was making the calls and screwing up the courage to listen to all the "Thanks, but no thanks" replies that were inevitable. Growing up, Jan had not been a person who was used to hearing, "no."

With so few appointments, she made virtually no sales. Her company data base sales-closing rate predicted one sale for every ten appointments, a number of appointments that many of her fellow advisors reached in a few days. She was lucky to have ten appointments in two months!

She was on the verge of quitting, and in fact, when her boss asked her to stop by the office for a "chat" she decided the option of quitting would be a moot point, as she was certain she was going to be terminated. Not without reason, either, she reminded herself.

But the visit was something else—an invitation to participate in the new advisor "EmoComp" sessions—training in emotional intelligence for new financial advisors. Surprised and again fighting back tears as they reviewed her miserable performance, she listened to her boss's pitch for the training and decided, why not? She would at least sit in, as it was better than getting beaten up on the phone every day and going home crying. Given that she was an apparent flop at this job, at least she could put the training on her resume.

This was Jan's state of mind at the time, she recalled, as she told me her story. What a difference today, ten months after that fateful visit to the boss's office. Her eyes sparkled as we talked, not now with tears but with the energy of her renewed faith in herself. At the time of our meeting, she had moved up ten places in her productivity ranking and was pushing hard against top ten overall. Her assets under management (a key performance metric) had swelled dramatically, an enviable record for anyone with her short tenure.

The training had been fantastic. She related how she mastered the techniques taught for mentally reframing "failure" reactions into simply non-personal and unthreatening information. She talked of her practice sessions, the feedback she got from her boss, and of the hours she spent reflecting on her emotions when she encountered similar rejections.

Over the weeks after the training, her appointment rate crept up; first 2 to 3 a week, then 5 to 6, then to her current average of more than 14 per week. In the first week after the training, she spent 16 hours making cold calls, almost 8 times what she had ever done before. Though she did not confirm a single appointment that week, she made it through all 16 hours of calling without breaking down and quitting. Using the techniques from the training that she eventually mastered, she persevered despite rejection. She managed her emotions and overcame her fears, making call after call after call until she scored her target level of "wins," and left to celebrate her success.

After our meeting, both of us feeling good, and with the sun bouncing off the Casco Bay waves, we rode to lunch in her venerable Porsche.

• • •

This was the story my evaluation efforts got for me about Jan. There was no doubt in her mind that this training had been successful, and there was little doubt in mine as well. I have always believed in the power of training. Despite my many struggles with evaluation methodologies and issues, I left the interaction with Jan absolutely convinced that, in her case, the emotional intelligence training her company provided had paid off, and paid off well.

Later, after getting the corroborating evidence and documentation I needed to verify her story, I reflected on the questions that nag so many in our field of training and development. Does training really make a difference? Can we "prove" impact? How can we make the business case for our investments in learning? What evidence can we collect that training really works?

Can We "Prove" Training Impact?

Jan's story is true, though her name and specific office location are fictitious. This was just one of several such stories my colleagues and I gathered during an evaluation of American Express Financial Advisors landmark training programs in emotional intelligence. Later in the book (Chapter Two) I will explain how collecting and verifying stories such as these fit into the Success Case Method evaluation process. In a moment, we will reflect on Jan's story and consider how it makes the case for training impact. But first it is useful to review the larger issue of training impact and how we have tried, in the past, to measure and evaluate it.

Training is one piece, and a small piece at that, in the larger puzzle of individual and organizational performance. The difficulties training professionals and their clients and critics have always had with measuring training benefits are that so many other factors are involved. A training program for sales representatives might indeed increase sales skills, but how much does it really contribute to increased sales and market share? If we measure sales records before and after training, we might or might not find any differences even if the training were having an effect. Or, we might find an increase in sales even if the training had not been any good. Market conditions, new competition, product characteristics, sales incentives, swings in the economy, and seasonal consumer demands are just a few of the factors besides the training that could easily influence bottom-line results. Given that so many other factors interact with the performance outcomes that training is aimed at, it becomes nearly impossible to sort out the effect that training did, or did not have.

This fundamental reality—that training is only one of many contributors to the goals that we seek to achieve from training—has been the major stumbling block for training evaluation. It has always been seen as relatively easy to measure the success of training when we look narrowly at whether people enjoyed it or believed it was a valuable experience. But so-called "smile sheets" do little to convince anyone that training is really worthwhile, since the enjoyment of training may have little or nothing to do with its ultimate success. It has also been relatively easy to test for learning outcomes, and say with confidence that people either did, or did not, increase their skill or knowledge as a result of a learning experience. But, did it really get used, and did using it lead to any worthwhile outcomes, and did the whole program make any lasting difference to important organizational outcomes such as revenues, competitive advantage, or profits? This has been the perennial impediment.

The training literature is full of evaluation methods and models that have sought to deal with the difficulties in measuring organizational training benefits and attributing these to the training intervention.

Experimental methods with randomized, double-blind treatment and control groups are considered the "gold standard" when it comes to determining the effects of interventions and making causal claims. But these are far too impractical and costly for use in the typical organizational setting.

- Quasi-experimental approaches, such as utility analysis (see Schmidt, et al, 1982, and also Cascio, 1989) or time-series designs (see, for example, Trochim, 1986). These methods are very complex, require sophisticated research and measurement skills, and their statistical manipulations and reports are difficult to comprehend.

- Simpler methods such as the return-on-investment (ROI) methods made popular by Jack Phillips (Phillips, 2003). But even the ROI models and methods can be time consuming and expensive. More importantly, they leave many questions unanswered and involve statistical calculations and extrapolations that raise serious doubts among report audiences.

Overall, when it comes to "proving" that a large training intervention made a worthwhile difference to a company or agency, there are many methodological stumbling blocks and practical realities that can be overwhelming. It is no wonder that most learning and development practitioners have pretty much thrown in the towel and sought to avoid the issue, or sought to deflect attacks by critics with occasional impact and ROI studies. My colleagues and I were no different from thousands of other training professionals; we also struggled with these difficulties, but for us the issues were even more poignant, as we were seeking to be experts in the training evaluation field and also to make a living actually doing evaluations of training.

When we pose the training evaluation question as trying to measure the impact of a large training program for hundreds of employees on the ultimate goals of an entire organization, then the problem indeed seems complex beyond practicality and overwhelmingly difficult. But, what if we step back for a moment, and ask a simpler question? Take the limited instance of whether training made a difference for one single person. What would we want to know, and how and where might we look for answers? These were the questions we asked ourselves when we were in the process of inventing the Success Case Method (SCM), and we surprised even ourselves with the relative ease of solving this problem.

Immediately, by posing the problem as making a case for training impact from one individual trainee, we relieved ourselves of all sorts of statistical significance and extrapolation burdens and obstacles imposed by having to make generalizations to multitudes of trainees. To simplify things further, the standard for evidence and validity we set for ourselves was derived from the jurisprudence model, not the realm of experimental methods and reductionist analytic techniques such as calculation of means and standards deviations. We wanted evidence that would convince a normal working professional with no research expertise—making the case beyond a reasonable doubt—that training did, or did not, work successfully.

Demonstrating Impact, One Trainee at a Time

Assuming that one single person was the focus of our inquiry, we thought we would really only need to have answers to three pretty simple and fundamental questions to make the case for a training success:

1. What, if anything, did this person learn that was new?
2. How, if at all, did this person use the new learning in some sort of job-specific behavior?
3. Did the usage of the learning help to produce any sort of worthwhile outcome?

If we got positive answers to these questions that we could really believe, would we not have a credible and defensible answer to the impact question? That is, what if we could demonstrate—with convincing evidence—that a person really did learn something new, that they really did use this learning in some important job application, and that this job application led to a worthwhile outcome; would we not have a credible and defensible instance of impact from training? We certainly believed so, and this belief became the foundation for the Success Case Method (Brinkerhoff, 2003). If we could not come up with a credible approach to making the case that training had a true impact for one person, we certainly would make no further progress in crafting a training evaluation method that could work at the program and organization level.

Now of course there may be skeptics who would question the veracity of the one-person impact instance, and no doubt you the reader have already begun to ask question yourself. To resolve the very reasonable doubts that anyone would have, we must take our answers to the three questions beyond simple "hearsay" and confirm them with evidence. We'll also have to eliminate some alternative explanations, even if we do find some successful post-training performance improvement. What if, for example, a person did good things after training but didn't really use anything they learned in the training to do so? To explore these doubts, we will return to the story of Jan, our financial advisor, and consider what additional questions we would have to resolve to accept her story as a true and valid instance of training impact.

Table 1-1 captures these doubts and concerns in a systematic fashion and arranges them by the three basic questions that we used to focus our inquiry. For purposes of further discussing how believable the impact claims can be, the three basic questions have been changed from question form to positive statements, and personalized to Jan's story.

Table 1-1 Looking for Alternative Explanations

Basic Impact Claim	Alternative Explanation Questions to Be Resolved
1. Jan learned some new skills for coping with emotional reactions that were hindering her success in making cold calls.	Was emotional interference really the cause of Jan's inability to make more cold calls? Were the skills truly new or had she already mastered them? Were the skills learned in the training or did she get them from somewhere else?
2. Jan's usage of her EmoComp skills helped her persevere and make more cold calls.	Did Jan in fact make more cold calls? Did Jan use the learned skills or did she really use some other skills that did not come from her training? Did the use of the skills really make the difference in making more cold calls, or did something else—perhaps a job aid or an incentive—cause her to change her behavior? *(Continued)*

Table 1-1 Looking for Alternative Explanations (Continued)

Basic Impact Claim	Alternative Explanation Questions to Be Resolved
	Could she have made more calls without the training, for instance if her boss had just told her to do it "or else"?
3. Jan's making more calls led directly to her making more appointments, which in turn led to her increase in sales.	Did Jan's sales performance really increase?
	Were the calls necessary to her getting more appointments?
	Did something else change that helped her get more appointments, such as better prospects on her call lists?
	Were more appointments necessary to her making more sales? Did she do anything else new that helped her get more sales?

Any skeptics worth their salt would certainly want answers to these questions before they would be ready to agree that Jan's story represents a training success. Thus, we knew that if we were going to take her story before senior executives at American Express and stand behind it, we would need to get good answers to these questions. And this is exactly what we do in a Success Case study, as we'll see in later chapters (especially Chapter Eight on interviewing and Chapter Nine on conclusions to be drawn from SCM studies.)

Using the SCM, we systematically raise and test the answers to each of the questions in Table 1-1. We do this by asking questions directly to Jan, and if we need corroborating evidence we ask other people, such as Jan's boss or a peer. We also look for evidence that would substantiate claims of impact learning, performance, and outcomes in documents and records. In addition, we test alternative explanations, such as whether a change in office procedures or market conditions may lead to equally significant performance improvement.

If we find that Jan really learned and used something from the training, and we could not find evidence that any alternative explanation from Table 1.1 was valid, we have to conclude that this training probably did work. Jan really was performing more effectively, she took the training, she learned something useful in it, she used it on the job, and the training was a major contributor to her success. If the training were not a success, the only alternative explanation could be that Jan was sorely and deeply deluded, and further, we would have to believe that some sort of conspiracy was in place to alter office records and arrange for co-workers and her boss to give us blatantly false information. Because none of these explanations is plausible, we must come to the conclusion that the training was successful, at least in Jan's case.

But wait. Jan's training was not the only thing that helped her performance improve. Certainly we are not ready to make the claim that her training, and her training alone, was the sole cause for her improved performance, are we? After all, you read in her story how her manager encouraged her to participate in the training, and how she practiced her skills after the training, and how her boss gave her feedback on her efforts. Surely these played a role. Indeed, they did and do, and we must take them into account as well.

Accounting for Other Success Factors

One of the things we have learned in decades conducting evaluation studies and reviewing the research and theoretical literature on learning and performance is this: training alone is never the sole factor in bringing about improved performance, and is often not even the major contributor. Given this, we never try to make an impact claim for training alone. Nor do we try, as some popular evaluation methods and models do, to estimate, isolate, or tease out the difference that training alone might have contributed. There are strong reasons for this, both methodological and strategic, that will be made very clear in the Chapter Three.

We already know without any inquiry at all that training alone was not a sufficient cause. Certainly, there were other factors that played into Jan's success, not the least of which were her boss's support and coaching, and the follow-up materials she could and did access. But, as she so convincingly claimed, this training was a necessary and vital catalyst. It came at just the right time and saved her professional life. She was an asset now to her family, to her office, and to her customers. There is no way, no way at all, that this would have happened but for that training.

We will not try to make a claim about the percentage of impact that was contributed by Jan's training. Again, in Chapter Three we'll explain why there are sound methodological and strategic reasons for not making such estimates. Instead, we just want to be sure, beyond a reasonable doubt, that had Jan not participated in and learned from her training, it is highly unlikely that her improved performance and the benefits that accrued from it would have happened. In other words,
we are very content with being able to show that training made a difference, and an important difference, and that the training contributed to valuable outcomes.

In fact, the Success Case Method has the additional goal of pinpointing exactly what additional factors played a role in the success of the training, such as a manager's commitment or a new incentive. Training is always dependent upon the interaction of these other performance system factors in the improvement of performance. If we can find out not only that training made a worthy and necessary contribution, but also what other factors played the biggest role in its success, then we can not only "prove" training, but we can take some very effective actions to improve it. If, for example, we know that success such as Jan's cannot be accomplished without several sequential instances of some feedback from a boss or co-worker, then we can make sure in future iterations of that training that such factors get put in place. We can educate the people who control these factors to manage them so they can get the greatest performance return for their training investments. We take this argument further in the third chapter where we look closely at a strategy for evaluation and show how the Success Case Method can be leveraged for management and organization development.

From Individual to Program Impact

Obviously, the Success Case Method does not look for only one training success out of a whole program. But the principles we employ in making the case that training worked for a whole program are exactly those that are involved in making the case for impact with one individual. If we could do this well, then next we would tackle the issue of assessing multiple individuals and looking for broader indicators of impact. Certainly a basic corollary is true: if we thoroughly searched and could not find a single real success, then we could make a decisive judgment about the failure of the entire program.

There is another key reason for beginning with a discussion of making the case for the impact on an individual. All training impact begins with the individual. Consider the case of the EmoComp training at American Express, consider further (as was actually the case) that many hundreds of employees were enrolled in this program. Now consider that of these hundreds some went on to use their training in job performance much as Jan did, and some did not. The amount of organizational impact that this training program helps produce is a direct function of the number of individuals who end up using their learning in ways that make a contribution. The more people who are like Jan Westbourne, who find an impediment in their performance that is deriving from some emotional issue, and then take steps to resolve it using a tool from the training, then the more impact this training will have. Clearly, if no one uses his or her learning, then there will be no impact. If 50 use it as well as Jan did, then there is more impact than if only three do.

Organizational impact of training boils down to two rather simple dimensions: the numbers of people who use their learning, and the power of the ways that they use it. One person who uses learning in a very powerful job application that leads to huge results will produce more impact than ten people who use their learning in pallid and ineffectual ways. Likewise, 50 people using their learning in very powerful ways will produce more impact than one person using that training in an equally powerful way.

Given these rather simple constructs, we can decide how to evaluate the training. If we want to find out how much good a training program did, there are two things we have to know:

- How many individuals used their learning in ways that led to worthwhile outcomes?
- What is the value of the outcomes that these individuals helped achieve through using their learning?

The good news is that this is not an overwhelmingly complex task. When it comes to making a case for training impact in the case of only one person, as we have seen, the burden of proof is not terribly difficult to assemble. There is further good news in that, because of certain predictable distributions of training results, we don't have to track down every single individual who participated in the training and analyze their experience. If this were the case, we would still be evaluating the American Express training even though we started it over seven years ago, as many thousands of employees participated. Given that training has a predictable range of effects and that sampling methods allow convincing generalizations, and also that we have developed some highly effective ways of getting at the right samples, the Success Case Method ranks as not only one of the most convincing means for evaluating impact of training, but one of the most simple and practical.

In the next chapter we will explain in more detail exactly how the Success Case Method works, building the case for training impact (or lack of it), one individual at a time.

Chapter Two

How the Success Case Method Works: Two Basic Steps

The Success Case Method has two basic steps. First, we identify those few trainees who have been the most, and least, successful, and record the proportions in each category. Then we interview some of these extremely successful and unsuccessful trainees to understand, analyze, and document their stories. The concept is simple. If the training is working, then we should find people who have indeed used it to accomplish worthwhile results. The SCM finds these people (if they exist) and documents, objectively and with concrete evidence, the results they have achieved. If we cannot find anyone at all who has done anything remotely worthwhile with his or her training, then of course we have learned something valuable; discouraging, yes, but valuable, because we now know that something is very wrong and that the training is having no apparent impact.

Similarly, the SCM looks for those people with whom the training has been the least successful—those who have not used their learning at all, or those who have tried it but achieved no worthwhile results. There is much to learn from these people. Some of them are not successful because they did not really learn from the training, due to low motivation, a mismatch of their needs with the training goals, and so forth. But the far greater number of non-successes have typically encountered performance system factors (ill-timed scheduling, a non-supportive manager, lack of incentives, inadequate measurement and feedback, for instance) that have prevented them from using their training in an effective way. In fact, when we compare the experience of the most and least successful, we almost always find out that the very same factors are at work in the successes and non-successes. Non-success, for example, may be explained in many instance, by the lack of support of a manager, while high success will likewise be explained by a very supportive manager.

Training Evaluation Realities

There are two realities about training programs that must be recognized and effectively dealt with because they dramatically influence the way we should think about and conduct evaluation of training. With the SCM, we not only recognize these realities to cope with them, but we very purposefully leverage them. The first reality is predictable results, which we will discuss before moving on to the second reality.

Reality One: Predictable Results

In our experience evaluating hundreds of training programs, we have noticed a familiar and consistent phenomenon, so obvious it is easy to miss: Training programs produce very reliable results. Imagine that you had conducted some training in a typical organization for several hundred people. Then, a few weeks or months after the training you followed up to find out how many people were using their training. Here is what you would be almost certain to find:

Some people have used their learning in ways that get great results. Some have not used their learning at all.

The large bulk of remaining others have tried some parts of it but noticed little if any changes or results, and eventually went back to the ways they were doing things before.

Almost never have we seen a program where absolutely everyone used their learning and got good results. Likewise, almost never have we seen a training program where absolutely everyone failed to use their learning at all.

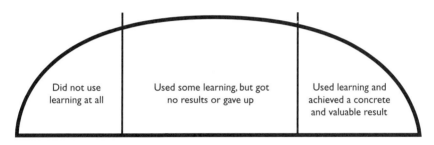

| Did not use learning at all | Used some learning, but got no results or gave up | Used learning and achieved a concrete and valuable result |

Figure 2-1   Predictable Distribution of Training Impact

Figure 2-1 depicts the predictable distribution of training success. We would not have to collect a shred of data to know what we will find after large numbers of people have been put through training: some will use it and get results, some will not, and everyone else is spread throughout the middle. There are usually a few people—sometimes many in the best instances—who find a way to put their training to use to lead to extremely valuable results, such as increased sales or improved quality. On the other hand, typically a small percentage (sometimes not so small) of people for one reason or another, are not able to use their training at all, or don't even try to use it. The bulk of trainees are distributed between these extremes.

We can learn a lot from inquiring into the experience of these ex-treme groups. An SCM study can tell us, for example, how much good a training initiative produces when the learning it produces is used in on-the-job performance. If the good that it produces is a great deal of good, such as when some trainees use their learning in a way that leads to highly valuable business results, then we know that the training had great potential for a high return on investment. In one case, for example, we found that just one trainee had used some leadership training to achieve business results valuable enough to pay for an additional three hundred people to go through the training. A second sort of typical SCM study result likewise has great strategic importance. When we find that the training produces really worthwhile results, but that it worked this well with only a very small number of trainees, then we can construct a defensible business case for investing time and resources to extend the good results to more people, as we did at American Express and many times elsewhere. Leveraging the knowledge gained from the few most successful trainees to help more trainees achieve similar levels of success is a key goal of a SCM study.

Tyranny of the Mean   Most traditional quantitative research methods are based on mathematical procedures that reduce large amounts of data to a few presumably meaningful statistics. Most common among these is the calculation of an arithmetic mean or "average" effect. Whenever we have a range of effects and calculate a mean, those scores at the high end will be offset by those at the low end. Imagine, for example, that we had ten high scores of 50 and ten low scores of zero. To calculate a mean we add all the scores together (for a total of 500) and divide by the number of scores (20) to calculate a mean of 25. We would also have a mean of 25 if we had a set of 20 scores and each score was 25. From the perspective of looking at the mean score, both of these sets of scores look the same, even though they are quite dramatically different.

If we apply this same example of a mean score to two different training programs, we can see how misleading a mean score can be. Imagine that for Training Program A there were ten very successful trainees who used their training and produced outstanding results and ten trainees who did not use their training at all. Compare this to Training Program B where all 20 trainees made use of their training, but only in a mediocre and marginally impactive way. Looking at the mean, both of these training programs look about the same; they both got mediocre results, on average. But the reality is that Training Program A has great potential that led to highly impactive results, but only for half the trainees. Training Program B, on the other hand, shows no such promise; it achieved only mediocre results for everyone and no one got good results. Training Program B is probably not worth keeping, but Training Program A appears to be very worthwhile, especially if we could figure out a way to get more than half the people using it as well as the top half did.

This "tyranny of the mean" effect is very powerful and at the same time very dangerous. Imagine, for instance, that some new visitor to America asked, "How is the food in New York City?" Answering honestly, you'd have to say that, on average, it was only mediocre. But of course, the reality is that there are some outstanding restaurants in New York City, as well as some pretty bad ones. Most everything—restaurants, automobiles, marriages, and children—is, on average, mediocre. For another example of the misleading nature of the mathematically reduced average, imagine that you are standing with one foot in a bucket of boiling water, and the other foot in a bucket of ice. Mathematically speaking, on average you are comfortable, though your true condition is anything but that.

Because most research and evaluation over the years have relied on traditional quantitative methods that use reductionist techniques such as means and mathematical averages, most training programs have over the years been assessed as having only mediocre effects. On average, it is true that most training does not work very well. But some programs work very well with some of the people, and this represents their great potential for being leveraged for even greater results.

To avoid the tyranny of the mean and to leverage the reality of the predictable results of training, we intentionally avoid seeking an "average" score and instead look deeply into the highest and lowest successes, for this is where the lessons about the true nature of the training's impact—and its potential for greater impact—lie.

Reality Two: Training Alone Never Works

Training and performance improvement practitioners wanting to evaluate their success have struggled for decades with the seemingly intractable issue that "other factors" are always at work with training. In a sales training program, for example, we might see an increase in sales, or we might not. How do we know it was the training that led to increased sales or the failure to get increases? Maybe it was some other factor, such as a change in the market, a new incentive to sell more, or something else. As we noted in the case of Jan Westbourne in the first chapter, there were a number of non-training factors that enabled her successful results from the training. Supervisory support, incentives, opportunities to try out learning, and the timing of the training, to name a few, are examples of the sorts of non-training or performance system factors that determine whether and how well training works to improve performance. The reality is, of course, that training alone never is the sole cause of a success or a failure. There is always something else at work that interacts with the training, and enhances its effects or impedes them.

A corollary of this reality is the fact that, when training works or does not work, it is most often the case that the non-training factors account for more of the success than features and elements of the training intervention or program itself. This reality again shapes the Success Case Method and allows us to leverage evaluation into truly valuable information.

Imagine for purposes of illustration that we had identified and evaluated one thousand training programs that failed to lead to worthwhile results. Almost all of the trainees in these programs, for one reason or another, did not ever use their learning in any ways that led to any worthwhile results.

Now imagine further that we have conducted an in-depth analysis of all these one thousand training programs that failed to get results and we know exactly why they failed; we have pinpointed all of the causes for their lack of impact. Finally, consider that we had further partitioned all of these causes for failure of impact into two categories:

Failures of the training intervention itself: these are causes such as a flawed instructional design, a poor instructor, ineffective delivery of the training, poorly designed materials, or other similar causes that prohibited the trainees from sufficiently mastering the learning objectives.

Failures of the training context: these are causes such as the wrong people attending the training, trainees attending who were not adequately prepared to learn or modify their behavior, a workplace that gave them no opportunity to practice the new skills, lack of managerial support, lack of incentives for changing job behavior to apply the new learning, and so forth.

This second reality of training evaluation means that most—probably as much as 80% or more—of the failures of training to achieve results are not caused by flawed training interventions, they are caused by contextual and performance system factors that were not aligned with and were otherwise at odds with the intended performance outcomes of the training. Thus, when we evaluate "training" impact, we are most often in reality evaluating an organization's performance management system.

In common practice, the way that this reality is often dealt with is to avoid it because it is so hard to measure and account for all these factors. So, we evaluate only the training itself, asking whether it appeared to be useful in the eyes of participants, and sometimes going so far as to measure whether people actually learned anything. Going beyond this to measure application of learning has typically not been very productive. First, surveys of learning application produce discouraging results, showing quite predictably that most trainees have not applied or sustained use of their learning. Secondly, when we discover that the majority of trainees are not using their learning in sustained performance, there is little the typical training department staff can do with this information, because they have no control over the performance system factors that are keeping the training from having a higher rate of application. Changing the training program will not do much if anything to get better results either, so the end result is that these surveys of training application end up being very unproductive.

The Success Case Method readily recognizes that these other-than-training performance system factors are hugely influential in helping to produce impact. But we make no attempt to partial out or otherwise isolate the training-related causes or to make any training specific causal claims. Instead, we seek one successful and unsuccessful trainee at a time, to identify all of the major factors that helped or hindered their achievement of worthwhile performance results from training. We can then build on and leverage this knowledge into recommendations for increasing performance in later iterations of training efforts. We discovered in the American Express example, for instance, that almost all new advisors who were successful in applying their learning and getting good financial results had also made use of additional resources that helped them practice new emotional competence skills on the job. We also discovered that nearly all of the successful advisors sought and received feedback from a manager or peer. This led us to conclude that the training was very unlikely to get any positive results without such additional interactions. This led in turn to recommendations to future trainees and their managers to be sure to provide time and opportunity for such assistance, as without it the training was likely to be ineffective and mostly wasted.

This acknowledgement of the inevitable interaction of training and non-training factors that produces results from training is a central part of the SCM approach. In fact, the SCM springs in part from a belief that efforts to isolate the effects of training are not just ineffectual, but that they are counter-productive and serve in the long run to undermine training effectiveness. We return to this issue in more depth in Chapter Three which explains a strategy for SCM application.

Leveraging the Two Realities

The Success Case Method, as we noted, begins with a survey to determine the general distribution of those training graduates who are using their learning to get worthwhile results and those who are most likely not having such success. In the second stage of a SCM study, we conduct in-depth interviews with a few of these successes and non-successes—just enough of them to be sure we have valid and trustworthy data. The purpose of the interviews is two-fold. First, we seek to understand, analyze and document the actual scope and value of the good results that the apparently successful people have claimed from the survey phase. This allows us to verify the actual rate of success, and also gauge its value. In a SCM study of sales representatives, for example, we were able to determine that the actual rate of success was about 17%; that is, 17% of the trainees who completed the training actually used their new learning in sustained and improved performance. Further, we could determine that the results they achieved were of a known value, in this example the typical results were worth about $25,000 per quarter in increased profits from sales of products with more favorable margins. (In later chapters we provide more detail about exactly how these impact estimates are made and verified).

Secondly, in the interview phase we probe deeply to identify and understand the training related factors (use of certain parts of the training or particular tools taught in the training, for instance) and performance system factors (supervisory assistance, incentives, feedback, and so forth) that differentiated non-successes from successes. We know that when the training works, it is likely that it has been supported by and interacted with certain replicable contextual factors. Knowing what these factors are enables us to make recommendations for helping subsequent trainees and later versions of the training initiative achieve better results.

Putting information from both of these SCM phases together creates highly powerful and useful information. First, we know what rate of success the training had, and the value of that rate in terms of the nature of the results that successful trainees were able to achieve using their learning. This lets us extrapolate the unrealized value of the training initiative—the value that was "left on the table" by the program due to its rate of non-success instances. This concept is graphically portrayed in Figure 2-2.

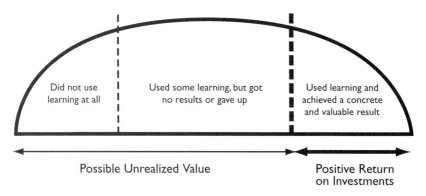

Figure 2-2   Proportion of Training that Represents Unrealized Value

This figure, very similar to Figure 2-1 shown earlier, represents a typical distribution of training results, showing a smaller proportion of trainees who used their learning and achieved positive results, and the larger percentage of those who did not achieve worthwhile results. Added to this figure is a notation of that proportion of the distribution that represents a positive return on the training investment (ROI), and that proportion of it that had no such positive return. The area above the darker and solid-line arrow shows that the trainees in this portion of the distribution achieved a positive ROI. We assume for purposes of this illustration that the value of the positive results in this portion of the distribution is indeed greater than the cost of providing and supporting the training for these people depicted in this portion. That is, whatever was spent to train the people who are represented in the solid-line area of the distribution was exceeded by the value of the results they achieved. However, everything to the left of this dividing line represents a loss or negative ROI. These people in the area above the thinner dotted line were trained, but did not use their learning in ways that led to positive results.

Given this, if there were ways to "grow" and make larger the area of the distribution above the solid-line arrow, then the return on investment would be greater. If we doubled, for example, the number of people who used their learning and got positive results, then we will have clearly dramatically increased the overall ROI of the training, since the costs for training all of the people in the distribution are roughly the same for each individual. Or, looked at in another way, the distribution to the left of the solid-line arrow area represents the potential unrealized value of the training. One of two basic explanations accounts for the distribution to the left and to the right of the darker dotted line.

Explanation #1: The training achieved its maximum possible value and got results from all of the people possible. It was 100% effective with all the people with whom it could have possibly worked. That is, only the trainees represented in the far right-hand portion of the distribution could have learned from and used their training, and all of those to the left-hand side were inherently incapable of learning or using this training at all (for example, they were not smart enough or not physically capable).

Explanation #2: There are some trainees to the left of the heavily dotted line who probably learned from and were capable of using their training, but something got in their way, such as a lack of opportunity or a non-supportive supervisor. Maybe there are some people to the left of the heavily dotted line who are not capable of learning or of using their training, but there are probably many more who could have made good use of it if they had received some of the support, and so forth, that those in the high success group received.

We typically assume that the second explanation is far more likely and we proceed forward on that assumption. If in our interview process we learn otherwise, of course we report that fact. But, as has always been the case in our many studies, we find that there is a large number of trainees that could have used their training more profitably but some obstacle kept them from doing so. Therefore, we conclude that there is unrealized value from the training; then we try to determine what the organization would need to do to improve the value and impact rates of future iterations of the training.

This lets us make a business case for growing the far right-hand side of the distribution in Figure 2-2. We can ask, for instance, what the value would be if we could grow the number of successful application instances by 10%. Then, we can ask what it might take to attempt this, for example getting more managers to support the training or getting more trainees to use the same job-aid as their successful counterparts did. We revisit this strategic goal of the SCM in greater depth in Chapter Three, and likewise in later chapters provide more detail and examples of exactly how we make the estimates and extrapolations presented briefly here. At this point it is useful to point out, however, that the methods and rules we use to draw these conclusions are not based in obscure or controversial statistical gyrations; rather, they are concrete and logical methods that are highly convincing. Our aim always is to use and present evidence that would "stand up in court," for anything less invites debate, argument, and doubt that is counterproductive to our purposes.

We should also point out that it is not always necessary to make conclusions about impact in terms of dollar values. We used such values in the preceding example only to make the case simple and clear. But we provide plenty of examples and instances where programs that do not entail such simply translated results can likewise benefit greatly from SCM methods.

This, in a nutshell, is how the SCM works. First, a survey (or sometimes another information harvesting method) is used to gauge the overall distribution of reported success and non-success. This is followed by an in-depth interview phase where we sample cases from each extreme of the distribution and dig deep to understand, analyze, and document the specific nature of exactly how the training was used and exactly what verifiable results it led to. As we will show in later chapters, this sampling and interview process is very robust and precise. Our aim is to discover, in clear and inarguable terms, exactly how the training was used (if it was) and exactly what value (if any) it led to. The standard of evidence is the same as we would use in a court of law: it must be provable beyond a reasonable doubt, documentable, verifiable, and compelling.

From this, we are able to conclude the following:

- When training works, what value does it help achieve?
- How frequently and at what rate does it work this well?
- When it works, why? What factors help or hinder results?
- What is the value lost by training not working?
- What is the case for making it work better?
- What would it take to make it work better; would such efforts be worthwhile?

Before we leave this chapter, we briefly present each of the major steps involved in carrying out a Success Case Method project. Following chapters dig more deeply into each of these steps, providing guidelines, tools, and examples for carrying out each step.

The Success Case Method: Step by Step

The two major phases of the SCM can be broken down into five (5) steps, as listed below.

1. Focus and plan the evaluation

2. Create an Impact Model that defines potential results and benefits

3. Design and conduct a survey to gauge overall success versus non-success rates

4. Conduct in-depth interviews of selected success and non-success instances

5. Formulate conclusions and recommendations, value, and return-on-investment

Step One: Focus and Plan the Evaluation

In the first step, the evaluator(s) think through what will be required to conduct an effective study that will provide the information people need and expect. The principal aim of this step is first to clarify and understand what the study needs to accomplish, and then identify and organize all the necessary elements of the study, so that the promise of the study will, in fact, be delivered.

Detailed and practical guidance about implementing this step of the Success Case model is provided in Chapter Four.

Step Two: Create an Impact Model

The impact model is a concise portrayal of the intended and potential outcomes of the training program that will be the focus of the SCM inquiry. This model identifies the job roles of the program participants and, for each job role, defines the particular on-job applications that each might make of the learning provided by the training. The model goes on to project the likely results of these applications of learning, and finally links these to the business goals and needs of the organization. The impact model provides the basis for and helps focus both the survey and interview portions of the SCM inquiry.

Chapter 5 provides in-depth explanations and examples related to the construction of impact models.

Step Three: Design and Conduct a Survey

The purpose of the survey is two-fold. First and foremost, we use the survey to identify the most, and least, successful users of training. In other words, we will use the survey response data to select candidates for in-depth interviews to analyze and document the nature and value of success. The second purpose of the survey is to assess the range and scope of successful learning applications. That is, we want to gauge the breadth of application and positive results among the participant population, being able to determine the numbers and proportions of trainees who represent the several categories of success and non-success.

Chapter Six deals with designing and conducting SCM surveys, and Chapter Seven provides guidance for how to analyze survey results.

Step Four: Conduct the Success Case Interviews

The Success Case interviews produce the data that are at the heart of the SCM: the stories of success, lack of success, and the factors that contributed to the participants' results. Sometimes, depending on the nature of the training program and its intended outcomes, there are several interviews conducted to analyze and document each Success Case. When, for example, we conducted an SCM inquiry of dealerships for a Big Three automobile company, we conducted interviews with sales representatives, sales managers, and business managers of certain dealers to thoroughly understand and document the success of a satellite television training initiative. The interview process includes planning and designing the interview process and protocol, training interviewers (if necessary), scheduling, preparing for and conducting the interviews, and analyzing the interview data to produce concise summaries of key impact features and factors.

Planning, conducting, and interpreting the Success Case interviews are addressed in Chapter Eight.

Step Five: Formulate Conclusions and Recommendations

The goal of this step is to determine key findings or "facts" that the data tell us, as well as the conclusions we can draw from them. We formalize conclusions about the impact the training contributed to, the scope and range of success across different categories of job roles involved in the training, and the value and significance of any unrealized value. This step typically also includes arriving at the recommendations for improving the impact of this training program, and for learning initiatives in general within the organization.

Chapter Nine addresses this step, focusing on establishing plausible evidence for claims that training was a principal cause of results and also defining the several types of SCM conclusions.

In sum, designing and implementing a Success Case study may be quite simple or relatively complex, depending on the overall scope and purpose of the initiative. We have conducted Success Case studies, for instance, that were planned, designed, implemented, and completed in a period of about three weeks, consuming fewer than 30 or so hours of our time in total. We have also conducted SCM studies that spanned half a year from start to finish and involved several hundred hours from a number of staff.

At the smaller end of the scale, we followed up just seven pharmaceutical sales representatives who were trying out some new methods and tools for soliciting business with health maintenance organizations (HMO's). At the other extreme, one of our Success Case projects looked at the impact of management development for an international child adoption and community development agency involving field office managers from dozens of countries around the globe, most in very remote and rural areas. Success case interviews were conducted in-person at several agency office locations. Given the remoteness of sites, our staff had to travel for several days get into the office locations (in one case by donkey when a rural bus broke down).

Regardless of their complexity and scope, all Success Case studies follow the major steps discussed in this chapter. The steps may be different, as more complex studies generally have more complex processes and tools, but each step will adhere to the purpose it intended to achieve.

Chapter Three

Success Case Method Strategy—Building Organizational Learning Capacity

*W*al-Mart and K-Mart are in the same business of selling consumer goods at discount prices. Both organizations also use information technology tools (i.e., computers, servers, etc.) in their operations. They each have essentially the same technical tools and capability. Their stores are highly similar, located in similar neighborhoods (sometimes adjacent to one another), they carry many of the same products, and they use virtually the same floor layouts and configurations. Yet one organization—Wal-Mart—is entirely dominant in its industry and has established superior competitive advantage. How? Wal-Mart uses its information technology differently, creating systems and processes for inventory, purchasing, distribution, and merchandising that lend it great competitive advantage, enabling it to sell goods at lower prices and stock stores more quickly and with less cost. The difference in the success of these two organizations lies not in the nature of the technology they use, but in how they make use of it.

There is a lesson here for organizational training and development. All organizations have essentially the same training technologies and tools available to them. In leadership development, for example, some use home-grown programs, some use programs from Vendor A and some use programs from Vendor B, and so forth. But if we were to take all of these leadership development programs and examine them side-by-side, there would be very few differences other than minor cosmetic and organizational features. While the training programs themselves are largely the same, organizations get dramatically different results from using them.

One company might use a popular vendor's program and get a lot of application of learning and resultant impact, while another similar company uses the same program and gets no impact at all. Even within the same organization, we see differences. One unit or division might get good impact while another gets little or none.

Over the years, as the use of vendor-supplied training became more common, we saw this phenomenon expand. Because we had contracts with some of these vendors to do impact evaluation studies, we might conduct ten or more impact evaluations of exactly the same training program in different organizations. What we found initially was baffling: the same program conducted by the same facilitators using exactly the same materials, in similar companies with similar personnel, would achieve dramatically different performance results. One company got great results, another got hardly any at all. How could this be?

The Determinants of Training Impact

Getting improved performance from the capabilities of employees is essentially a performance management challenge. Whether employees perform to the best of their ability or at some level less than their best ability is driven by a complex host of factors, typically and popularly lumped together under the rubric of the "performance management system." While these factors may not be organized or even viewed as a systemic entity, they nonetheless operate as a system, either suppressing or enhancing employee performance. Incentives, for example, play a role in whether people perform effectively. Direction, whether people know what it is they are supposed to do, is another important factor. Together, factors such as direction, feedback, incentives, rewards, and job aids and tools, all work together to shape and drive performance. When these factors are effective, complete, and aligned, employee capability will be leveraged into superior performance. When they are not, performance will consistently be degraded to levels far below employee capability.

Learning Alone Is Insufficient

Impact from training is a function of a high-quality training intervention that operates in conjunction with a healthy, aligned, and integrated set of performance system factors. The principal requirement for the training program is that it must efficiently and effectively help participants acquire new and robust skills and knowledge that are important for adopting new job behaviors or improving effectiveness of current job behaviors. Imagine, for example, an organization that is implementing new software systems as part of an effort to provide more effective customer service. Imagine further that the new software requires new skills and knowledge on the part of customer service representatives, such as how to complete an electronic customer service request on-line, and how the new system can be accessed to reduce customer waiting time. In this example, the training must help participants fully understand the features of the new system and how they can be leveraged, and it must help them master certain skills in using the system to effectively complete certain key job tasks.

But whether the training leads to any worthwhile impact, such as real improvements in customer service or reduced waiting time for service will be determined by how much and how well service representatives actually use this learning on the job in improved job performance. It is possible, for example, that a service representative could fully achieve the immediate outcomes of the training program, but end up being impeded from ever using this learning on the job. If, for an obvious instance, the computer system at this person's job site was flawed and the software didn't work, then clearly there would be no favorable impact. Or, if the service representative's supervisor was not in favor of the system, then this supervisor might influence the person not to use it. Or, for yet another example, it might be that using the system initially takes longer because of other work pressures on the job, and that this newly trained person, out of frustration, reverts to the old way of providing service. In sum, any number of these and other factors, alone or in combination, could be very likely to impede the impact of this training despite how well the training worked to produce the desired new skills and knowledge.

The reality is that these non-training, performance system factors are the principal determinants of impact from training and can, if they are not aligned and integrated, easily overwhelm even the very best training. Research on training impact (see, for example Yukl & Tannenbaum 1993; Tessmer and Richey 1997) convincingly documents the potency of these factors, as do our evaluation experiences, and the anecdotal experience of thousands and thousands of learning professionals. Best estimates are that probably 80% or more of the eventual impact of training is determined by performance system factors, while the remaining 20% or so is driven by the quality of the training intervention itself and the characteristics of the earner, such as inherent ability and motivational values.

The fact that the training intervention itself is a smaller contributor to the overall impact formula cannot be construed as a license to ignore training program quality. Producing learning outcomes effectively and efficiently is a must, a precondition and a necessity for impact. But in our experience, the state of training practice is such that, for the most part in most organizations, training interventions are typically of reasonably high quality. When they are not, of course, they must be singled out and revised. We have seen our share of inferior training programs, and there are improvements that could be made to almost any training program as well. But when it comes to seeking leverage for improvements, it is most often the case that an ounce of performance system enhancements will lead to many pounds of improved impact from training, while making improvements in an already suitable learning intervention is unlikely to yield dramatic improvements in impact, especially in the face of a flawed performance system environment.

Our vast experience in evaluating training programs and the conclusions of many research studies on training transfer and impact all lead to the same conclusions: the principal barriers to achieving greater application of learning and subsequent business results lie in the performance environment of the trainees, not in flaws (though there may be some) in the training programs and interventions themselves[1]. Participants that are

1 These observations and the research on training programs apply to training as it is typically designed and implemented in most organizations, for example as one-time seminars, workshops, and the like. One can make a very worthy argument that more comprehensive training "programs" would not fall prey to such low rates of impact. Initiatives that were extended over weeks or months and included performance technology tools and methods, such as incentives, job aids, and coaching and measurement feedback from supervisors would be far more effective. The Advantage Performance Group (APG), Pitney Bowes, and Midland Insurance, among other companies we know of, regularly conduct training initiatives that employ these impact-enhancing methods. They find these approaches achieve dramatically improved performance and business outcomes. Several of these organizations further employ SCM studies as part of their efforts to suggest further impact-enhancing improvements, again with great success.

involved in training usually have sufficient innate abilities to master the learning outcomes. Similarly, they also typically have sufficiently positive values that are supportive of the aims of training. Most care about their work and, given the right opportunities, will want to improve. There are of course, exceptions to this. Most companies have at least some minority of employees who should not have been hired in the first place and who do not have the innate ability to succeed. But, these are in the vast minority. The typical training program, for example, leads to less than a 15% success rate. It would be a highly unusual organization indeed that could blame this low rate of impact on the learners, claiming that 85% of its employees are too stupid to be able to master and apply required new skills.

Motivation to learn is another matter and can account for a significantly larger proportion of failed results from training. But, on closer consideration, it is again very rare that one would find an employee inherently indisposed to learning. Far more often, poorly motivated employees have developed this negative outlook because of a poorly constructed performance system and workplace culture. Thus, the larger part of poor motivation to learn and perform more effectively can be countered by concomitant changes in the performance environment, such as better trained supervisors, more effective incentives, more effective feedback and direction, more clear and consistent consequences for poor performance, and so on.

Risks of the Common Training Evaluation Strategy

The bulk of evaluation methods and models in use today derive from the original Kirkpatrick (1967) four-level framework and are construed conceptually as if "training" were the object of the evaluation. Improving the quality and enjoyability of a wedding ceremony may reap some entertaining outcomes for wedding celebrants, but this would probably do little to create a sustained and constructive marriage. But we in the training profession continue to rely on evaluation methods and models that evaluate the wedding—a training program—when what we need is a more productive marriage—sustained performance improvement that adds value.

A training-focused evaluation strategy poses three essential and significant risks:

- It undermines performance partnerships with line management by misrepresenting the role and process of training in performance improvement.
- It ignores the performance system factors that impinge on training impact.
- It fails to provide accurate and relevant feedback that managers—the customers of training—need to guide performance improvement.

Risk One: Traditional Impact Evaluation Undermines Management Partnerships

Senior and supervisory management own the many performance system factors that threaten results. Given this fact of performance life, training practitioners have worked hard to forge a partnership strategy with other key participants in the organization, such as line managers, human resource executives, and other senior leaders. As these others hold the keys to the performance system, their active and cooperative participation is essential for training to work. The very essence of the partnership strategy is a clear message from training: We cannot do this alone. Without you (the rest of the key players), training cannot succeed.

But in the face of this plea for a partnership we find evaluation methods that seek to credit training for impact, and that do not recognize the vital contributions of the other players in the performance process. These methods are divisive and exacerbate the political isolation of the training function. Improving individual, team, and business performance must remain the central focus of training practitioners, and we must work doggedly to create the internal alliances necessary to work systemically. We cannot afford to send mixed messages about what it takes to accomplish our mission; nor can we afford to divert resources into evaluation initiatives that are not aligned with it.

Risk Two: Lack of Focus on Performance System Factors

The effects of the prevailing performance system are consistently powerful and predictable. Despite the fact that the greatest determinant of impact is the performance system, the four-level evaluation framework does not guide inquiry directly to the performance environment, nor does it aim to identify and assess the most critical performance factors that make the difference between success and failure. In other words, this sort of evaluation can be used to defend and take credit for behavioral change, but it provides no focused and explicit inquiry into what factors in the performance environment enabled or impeded that usage. Nor does it provide information that could be used to identify and recognize the key players who had a major role in the success or failure to achieve results.

Risk Three: Evaluation Feedback Goes to the Wrong People

Senior leadership and supervising managers are the owners of the performance environment. Senior management is responsible for the organizational structure, policies, and procedures that provide the overall performance system architecture. Supervising managers hold the keys to ongoing performance improvement because they are responsible for the day-to-day coaching and other performance management activities that most shape behavior. But the traditional four-level framework is conceived to provide feedback primarily to the training function, as if it alone were responsible for performance improvement, and essentially ignores the larger performance system.

If we want to evaluate "transfer" or behavioral change from training, we must evaluate the managerial and performance system, not training. The primary feedback channel should be to the owners of the performance system: line management and senior leadership. If we are really serious about improving the performance that training can contribute to, then we need to be equally serious about getting all the players in the performance partnership involved in understanding their roles, their contributions, their successes, and their failures. We will never be able to leverage improvements to transfer by creating and disseminating follow-up surveys that assess usage of learning, when the principal feedback channel is to the training function.

An Evaluation Strategy for Building Organizational Learning Competence

The central challenge for organizations today is how to leverage learning consistently, quickly, and effectively into improved performance. In the typical state-of-the-practice in the typical organization, this capability is extremely low. When training impact is defined as the application of new learning in job behaviors that produce or lead to valuable organizational outcomes, then the typical rate of impact from training is usually less than 15%. Given this very low rate, organizations and learning professionals don't need an evaluation method that keeps rediscovering this painful truth. Instead, they need a strategy and method for changing it. The SCM is, above all, such a method.

The overarching purpose of the SCM is to dig out and build understanding about the many factors that keep training from being more successful, then serve as a vehicle to teach the key stakeholders in the organization what needs to be done to turn the training success rates from their current miserably low rates of impact into consistently higher impact with consistently improving rates of return for training investments. Training today yields about an ounce of value for every pound of resources invested. The goal for the SCM is to reverse this recipe—to get a pound of value for an ounce of investment.

Given the distributed responsibility for creating and managing a supportive learning-to-performance environment, this is clearly a whole organization challenge, not one the training function can accomplish alone. If training has worked, it is because everyone on the performance management "team" has done things right. Providing feedback to the learning and development (L&D) department or function is partially useful, but cannot be the sole focus of evaluation, because there is little the training department can do to correct deficiencies in the performance system. The ownership and responsibility for the management of the performance system factors is spread among immediate supervisors of trainees, their managers, the owners of related systems (human resources, information systems, strategic planning, and so forth), and senior leaders. These other players in the organization have their hands on the levers that need to be manipulated in order to bring the performance system into alignment and make training work.

A Fundamental Shift in Focus

With the SCM, we shift the focus from evaluation of "training" to an evaluation of how effectively the organization uses training. Thus we evaluate how well the organization uses training systems and resources and leverages them into improved performance that in turn drives business results. This focuses inquiry on the larger process of training as it is integrated with performance management, and includes those factors and actions that determine whether training is likely to work to get performance results or not.

To assure this more systemic focus, the SCM adopts a conceptualization of the training process (Advantage Performance Group 2005; Brinkerhoff & Apking 2001) that suggests that we look at any training intervention as being comprised of three fundamental and interrelated segments as portrayed below in Figure 3-1

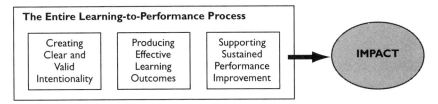

Figure 3-1 The Learning-to-Performance Process

In Figure 3-1, we define a learning-to-performance process whose three parts work together to produce the impact that the organization seeks, such as improved customer service, increased quality, reduced costs, and so forth. For training initiatives to be fully effective, all three parts of the larger process must be completely and effectively implemented, and further, the three parts must be aligned and integrated.

Creating Clear and Valid Intentionality

This portion of the process, when completed effectively, assures that all learning interventions are linked to worthwhile organizational goals and that managers and other leaders understand and are committed to them. It also means that individual learners who will be participants in the learning activities have defined and made a commitment to a "line of sight" between the learning outcomes the training can provide to them individually, one or more applications in their jobs, and thence in turn to one or more job results that these applications could achieve that would benefit either or both them and their work units.

Producing Effective Learning Outcomes

This portion of the process refers to what would typically be defined as the training program, such as a workshop, a seminar, or a class. This represents the learning intervention itself and includes all of the instructional activities in which trainees would engage to be sure they mastered the knowledge, skill, and attitudinal outcomes of the training program.

Supporting Sustained Performance Improvement

Learning is, we know, most fragile when it is new. If proper support activities are not in place, then it is likely that learners will not try out their new learning at all, or will quickly revert to their old, pre-training ways of performing. Thus, this portion of the process includes assuring coaching, feedback, incentives, reviews of action plans, manager support for new performance, and so forth.

All three of these process elements must be integrated and aligned for training to achieve consistently high rates of impact. When any part of these three process elements is flawed or does not work in alignment, then training impact is impaired. It is possible, for example, to conduct an excellent learning event that achieves no impact at all; in fact, L&D professionals witness this circumstance frequently, much to their chagrin. Imagine, for example, that before an employee participated in a training program that her supervisor only grudgingly allowed her to participate and expressed an opinion that this training was likely to be mostly a waste of time. Imagine further that when this employee completed the training program that the manager failed to provide any encouragement for using the learning, or worse yet, said this (or words to this effect):

"What a relief to see you are back from that training program. There's a lot of important work that's piled up since you were gone. We missed you! Let me know as soon as you're caught up so we can get back on track."

Note that there is not only no encouragement to apply any of the new learning, but there is an implicit message that the really important work is not anything new but the old ways that prevailed prior to the training. In this manager's view, the training was an unwelcome interruption of business as usual. Despite the quality of the training this employee attended and despite whatever new methods she learned, there is a very low likelihood it will be put to use. Most likely, after a week or two go by, this training will have faded out completely and it will be as if it never happened.

This manager's message is unfortunately far more common than not and illustrates one of the ways that the performance environment overwhelms the best intentions of training. The same message is sent, perhaps less explicitly, by entrenched behavior and belief patterns, rigid management practices and traditions, aversion to risk taking, rampant fear of change in workplace cultures, misaligned incentive systems, out-of-date information and measurement systems, and so on and on.

These many factors have to be pinpointed and brought into the light of inspection before they can be changed. A training evaluation approach that ignores them or simply reduces them to background noise against the assumption that the principal focus of inquiry is the training and learning event itself will never get any traction to reshape practice and make fundamental change.

Redefining the Evaluation Process

We define the SCM approach as a process that seeks out and identifies these key impact-determining factors, so that credit can be placed with and feedback provided to the credit-worthy parties. If the training has not worked, then the SCM likewise pinpoints the weaknesses in the system, and directs feedback to those who can do something about the problems. Above all, the SCM is intended to help all stakeholders learn what worked, what did not, what worthwhile results have been achieved, and most importantly, what can be done to get better results from future efforts. Again, we note that the focus of the SCM is not on "training" but on how effectively training is being used by an organization to achieve results.

The SCM evaluation approach is organized around three primary questions:

1. How well is our organization using learning to drive needed performance improvement?

2. What is our organization doing that facilitates performance improvement from learning that needs to be maintained and strengthened?

3. What is our organization doing, or not doing, that is impeding performance improvement from learning that needs to change?

These key questions are embedded in an evaluation strategy with the overall purpose of building organizational capability to increase the performance and business value of training investments. This strategy is essentially an organizational learning approach that is well aligned with the overall training mission, which is likewise to build organizational capability through learning. Implementing this evaluation strategy requires that evaluation focus on factors in the larger learning-performance process and that it engage and provide feedback to several audiences.

Figure 3-2 shows that evaluation inquiry is focused on the entire learning-performance process, from clarification of training needs and goals, to selection and preparation of learners, to their engagement in learning and on to the transfer and support of learning into workplace performance. Evaluation findings and conclusions are provided through multiple channels to the several owners of the impact factors unearthed by the evaluation, who then are encouraged to take action to nurture

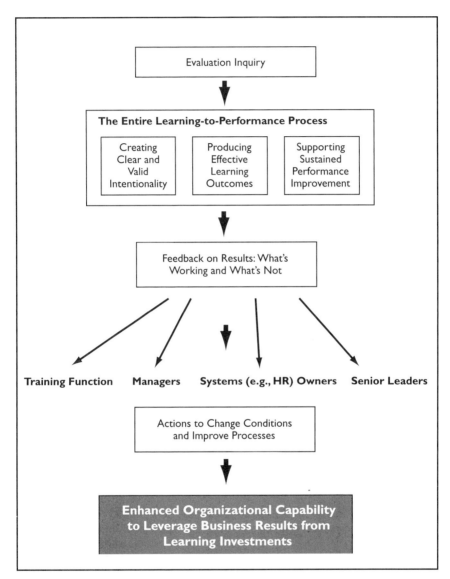

Figure 3-2 Success Case Method Evaluation Strategy

and sustain those things that are working and to notice and change those things that are not. The ultimate goal of this evaluation inquiry is the development of the organization's "learning capability": its capacity to manage learning resources and leverage them into continuously improved performance.

The bottom portion of the figure reminds us that evaluation has a clear and constructive purpose. It is not self-serving, it is not defensive, and it is not solely for the benefit of the learning and development (L&D) function. Like learning and performance services themselves, evaluation is another tool to improve performance and business results. This also reminds us that the line management side of the organization and the L&D function jointly share responsibility and leverage for this capability. No single party alone can assure success, nor can either alone take credit.

The performance improvement process has learning at its heart, but learning and performance are inseparable. Learning enables performance, and performance enables learning. Evaluation of training, when embedded in a coherent and constructive strategic framework like the one presented, is a powerful tool for organizational learning and capability building. It is not only consistent with the concept of shared ownership; it is a method for achieving and strengthening the partnership of learning and development professionals with the other key players in the performance and business improvement process.

Implementing the Strategy to Drive Change

In some respects, the entire remainder of this book is about implementing the SCM strategy as it deals in more detail with how to plan and conduct a SCM project. But at a higher level, it is useful at this point to explain the principal structure of the argumentation framework that comprises the SCM strategy as a driver of change to create an organization more capable of getting results from training investments. A typical SCM study aims to make three (3) related claims, each supported by compelling evidence.

Claim One: The Training, When It Works, Leads to Valuable Results

This is the first contention we pursue, seeking evidence of whether the training initiative has helped anyone achieve any worthwhile results. The scope of the impact is of less concern than is its value. That is, we are not so much concerned with determining whether a large proportion of trainees may have used their learning to achieve impact as we are with finding out how valuable the impact is that results from usage of learning. If there is little to no value from people using their learning, then the training may be aimed at needs with little business value, or it may be that training graduates have not yet discovered more impactive applications of their learning. In either case, there is no compelling evidence that the learning program is capable of helping to produce valuable results.

On the other hand, if only a small proportion of trainees have used their learning, but these applications have led to a great deal of worthwhile impact, then it makes sense to explore further the business case for extending that application to more people, thus milking more value from the training. In one case, for instance, our SCM study found only one trainee who had been able to apply learning, but that application led to sales increases worth more than a million dollars in revenues in just one quarter. There was no reason to believe that other trainees could not have done at least partially as well, so the hunt was on!

The first focus of the SCM process is to look for evidence of learning applications, then to assess the value of the results these applications may have led to. This first focus must also support the claim that the training was a necessary catalyst for achieving the results. If something other than the training was responsible for the results (that is, the training played no key role in the achievement of results) then the quest is likewise near an end. In any case, whether the training has helped achieve impact or not, the SCM evaluation has discovered useful information. In the case of no impact, of course, it is disappointing information and will not lead to the latter stages of strategic leverage, but certainly finding out that training that was supposed to work is not working is a very important discovery.

Claim Two: The Training Is Under-Leveraged and Could Achieve More Worthwhile Value

This claim grows from comparing the value contributed by the training to the proportion of those who applied their learning. If this proportion is large enough that nearly all the trainees used their learning and all of these applications led to highly worthwhile results, then the organization is clearly to be congratulated for this noteworthy accomplishment, and it would be important for the organization to consider whether there are other trainee populations with whom this training could work. Of course, the "everyone used it and everyone achieved great-results" scenario is not very likely. If training quite regularly worked this well, there would be no need for this book nor would you, the reader, be taking the time to read it—you would turn your attention to more important matters and problems.

The far more usual scenario is that a small proportion of trainees actually apply their learning, and further, that not even all of these applications of learning turn out to be worthwhile.

Assuming that there is firm evidence that the training works, even if only for a small percentage of people, and also that there is firm evidence that the training is a principal catalyst for the results, then we go on to explore the contention that more of the trainees could have used their learning to achieve the same, or close to the same results. We have to be sure that the training has not achieved its maximum possible value. It is possible, though unlikely, that the training could only have worked with this small proportion of the trainees, and that it was 100% successful with them. We examine this possibility and either reject or confirm it. (In fact, we have yet to encounter a circumstance where the unlikely scenario is true: that the training only worked with a handful of people and that there are no more that could have benefited from it.)

It is possible, though again unlikely, that the principal factor that enabled some people to apply their learning and that kept others from applying their learning lies with the inherent capabilities and characteristics of the trainees themselves. That is, maybe those who used the training are smarter, and those who did not are less smart. Or, those who used it had good attitudes and those who did not didn't care. But again, these explanations are unlikely. It is far more likely that the people who used it and those who did not are in most characteristics quite similar, but they are exposed to and work in different performance environments and workplace climates.

This is, of course, exactly the hypothesis we test in the SCM by seeking out those factors that differentiate high successes from lower successes. Most often, the causes are not only obvious but quite mundane. Below we list what we commonly find as the factors that differentiate those trainees who used their learning and got good results from those who did not. Trainees who got great results often shared these characteristics:

- They were provided or seized an opportunity to apply their learning soon after their training was completed.
- They had a clear and realistic expectation of what the training was about and already had identified one or more worthwhile possible applications.
- They had a manager who helped them prepare for the training and who supported their application of it.

- They were supported by incentives, rewards, and encouragement for supervisors, peers and others.

- They engaged in the training at the right time; close to a pressing need to use it.

- They had the tools and resources needed to apply the learning readily available to them.

On the flip side, trainees who did not apply their learning were exposed to the same sorts of factors but in a negative way. That is, their learning came at a bad time, they lacked an opportunity, they had a manager ill-disposed to provide support, and so forth. As noted, these are not mysterious and arcane factors but are quite typical and expected. Note also that these factors are malleable. They can be managed and ameliorated. This takes us to the third element of the change strategy.

Claim Three: Achieving Greater Value Requires Action on the Part of Key Players in the Performance System Environment

This third claim is where the leverage for change lies. If the training gets worthwhile results some of the time, and if it would be worthwhile getting more such results, then the argument can be made that it would be worthwhile to do something to make this happen. That is, we aim to make a business case for taking action to get more value from the learning program.

We might, for example, provide information that compares the value achieved in managers' work units where the training worked to the value achieved in those units where it did not. Say, for example, we can show (as we often do with the SCM) that managers whose direct reports tended to apply their learning experience had positive gains in business metrics while those whose direct reports did not apply their learning lost money on the training and failed to reap such positive business impact.

Now we are in a position to make a business case for taking action to improve the results of the training. That is, we can tell managers what they need to do to get more value from future iterations of the training, and what it would be worth to them if they did.

This final stage of the argument closes the strategy loop. It provides information that the organization can use to improve its results from learning investments, and provides data-based and organization-specific evidence to support this. Closing the feedback loop by showing stakeholders what value they gained or lost from training when it worked, telling them why it worked when it did work and why it did not when it didn't, and telling them further what needs to be done to make it work better and the value they would get from it when it works better is powerful stuff. It can get the change ball rolling, and this is exactly what we want if we are to make progress toward developing the truly learning-savvy organization that is increasingly capable of turning its learning investments into valuable performance and business improvement.

Chapter Four

Focusing and Planning a Success Case Method Study

*I*n Chapter Three we outlined the general framework and steps in completing an SCM study. However, it is important to keep in mind that each study has its own purpose and context, and the study design needs to reflect these unique elements. The purpose of this chapter is to enable a practitioner to think through all of the considerations that will shape a particular study—in short, to ensure that each evaluation has the best and most efficient design to achieve the study's purpose within the context of that specific organization.

There are eight key areas in which Success Case Method design decisions must be made:

1. The purpose of the study

2. The stakeholders (groups and individuals) who want or need the study to be done, and the importance of the study to each

3. The specific program or initiative on which the study will focus

4. Who the program's participants are and how many of them should be included in the study

5. How soon after the training the follow-up survey should be conducted

6. The schedule for the study

7. The resources that are available for completing the study

8. The overall strategy for the study that will work best

These decision areas are not necessarily pursued in a stepwise, linear fashion. But it is important to note that these decisions interact with each other. Practitioners will find that decisions in one area affect the understanding of and decisions in another area. For example, the initial understanding of purpose may need to be limited to accommodate the resources that are available for the study. Or, likewise, discussions with stakeholders may surface a time limitation that the study must accommodate, which will in turn limit the scope of the study to a particular portion of the program being investigated, unless an increase in resources can be negotiated.

The eighth decision area, the overall strategy for the study, may be an exception to the non-linear nature of study planning. The decision must be made last, as it is shaped by decisions in the other six areas. Once practitioners have addressed this eighth decision area, they have achieved the overall goal of Step 1.

1. Clarifying the Purpose of the SCM Study

A SCM study has the general purpose of determining the impact of a training program on its participants and the organization. The next question that must be asked is, "Who cares? Why should anyone bother to do this?" The answers to these questions enable the evaluation team to focus and design the study in such a way that ensures the stakeholders get the breadth and depth of information they need. For example, if a training department is being held accountable by the Vice President of Human Resources to demonstrate the return on investment of a sales training program, knowing this up front can help ensure that in the data collection process the evaluators probe in depth to quantify the impact of the training. In another case, a training project team may want to know how well the early stages of a large program roll-out are working. In a recent project, for example, a team from the Boeing company was responsible for a training program for engineering managers. Eventually, they would provide the training to more than 2,000 staff members. After the first 70 or so managers had completed the program, they planned an SCM effort to determine how well the program was working for this early group. This would enable the program team to make any necessary revisions to the program to enhance impact, but would also give them information about how future training audiences could gain the greatest impact.

Here is a list of some of the key purposes that the Success Case Method has been used to address.

- Documenting the nature and extent of impact to ensure that a training program is achieving its intended results

- Estimating the ROI of a program

- Creating examples of success for use in marketing a program or otherwise convincing others of its value

- Documenting the actions early adopters take to apply and get results from their training to guide and motivate latter participants

- Refining and improving a program based on the experience of those who have actually participated in it

- Assessing what a program is actually achieving to decide whether or not to continue it

- Documenting the actual impact of a program to allay (or confirm!) the concerns of skeptics
- Assessing the impact of a pilot program before making a decision to engage in a larger implementation effort
- Developing awareness of the contextual factors that support, or inhibit, successful applications of a program or innovation
- Helping make a business case for line managers to take a more active role in supporting, for example—through coaching and feedback—the way in which their employees apply training to achieve impact

This list of purposes is necessarily generic. In practice, each general purpose is further refined in interaction with key stakeholders. For example, in working with American Express Financial Advisors to evaluate their training program in emotional intelligence, the general purpose for our Success Case study was to assess and document impact. There was general agreement, based on sporadic anecdotal evidence, that the program was probably useful and was helping people achieve worthwhile results. But there were questions about whether the actual impact of the program was really worthwhile in light of what the overall business was hoping to achieve. Thus we refined our understanding of the purpose to be sure to search for and document highly conclusive and verifiable impact data.

2. Meet with and Discuss the Study with Key Stakeholders

A stakeholder is, as the name implies, a person or group that holds some "stake" in the study. This will include those who commission or will use the results of the SCM study such as program sponsors (who may be line managers) and training managers. Trainers and program "owners" are also stakeholders, as the results of the study may influence decisions about their program, even to the point of deciding that it may be a candidate for termination. Stakeholders also include program participants and especially their managers, potential participants and their managers, and others who would benefit or suffer a loss depending on the success of the program to be evaluated.

Once a study is underway it is difficult to accommodate the interests of a stakeholder who has been overlooked, so this task needs to be conducted before the SCM project takes final shape. In addition, it often happens that an ignored or overlooked stakeholder emerges later in a study to undermine it and its findings. Evaluations are intended to have consequences that can affect the stakeholders, in sometimes uncomfortable ways. For this reason evaluators have an ethical responsibility to thoroughly identify stakeholders and understand and consider their needs and interests in the planning stages of a study. Though the evaluation design may not be able to accommodate the interests of all stakeholders, the evaluation team should make decisions to not accommodate interests intentionally and with due consideration, not by default or oversight. In addition, just the process of listening to the needs and interests of stakeholders may win their support for the study.

Who the stakeholders are for a study and how they are involved in planning will usually depend on the scope and purpose of the study. If, for example, the study is of very limited scope, the number of stakeholders and their involvement in the study is often likewise limited and may be dealt with relatively casually.

3. Define the Program That Is to Be Studied

At the surface, one would think this task would be straightforward, especially as the evaluation team would have had preliminary discussions with the study's sponsors about the evaluation of a specific course. Defining the program is actually at times simple, as was the case with the small program for sales reps. Because only six reps had completed the training and the course was a simple electronic learning module, the scope and nature of the training were very simple to define clearly. However, at other times the evaluators have to clearly define the parameters of the program to be evaluated. For example, consider our assessment of the emotional intelligence training at American Express. In this instance, we were asked to use the SCM to measure the impact of American Express' "emotional intelligence training program." One of the first questions we needed to resolve was this: Exactly what is the "program"? Emotional intelligence training at American Express consisted of several training interventions, each with a variety of follow-up options, and each delivered in a variety of formats. These several variants included a five-day session for senior executives, a one-day introductory session (included in a longer two-week orientation) for newly hired financial advisors, and a three-day workshop for intact branch offices that could be customized by the corporate training office. There were also many other "one-off" sorts of presentations, orientations, and training sessions that the corporate training office had provided when none of the standard offerings were convenient. Finally, there were several on-line and videotaped modules, as well as a number of brief brochures and other written resources that employees could use in a variety of combinations. We decided, after considerable discussion with stakeholders, that for our evaluation purposes the "program" would be defined as three separate elements, each for a different audience: (a) the one-day session for new financial advisors; (b) the five-day workshop for executives; and (c) the three-day office workshop. Anyone else who participated in some other form of emotional intelligence training was not considered to be a participant in "the program." We chose only these three sessions to include in the program definition because they were the only variants in which any one session delivery was reasonably assured to be the same as another. We could have included all of the other variants, but because they involved only very limited audiences, and to keep SCM costs down, we included in our scope only the three major program options, and limited scope further to only those employees that had completed the program in the past 12 months.

The program to be studied must be defined, in clear terms that delimit—for all to understand—what is, and what is not, part of the program. Only then should the evaluation planning move forward to the next, related step, that of determining exactly what participant groups comprise the population of participants to be included.

4. Define the Population of Participants to Be Studied, and Identify Any Needed Sampling Parameters

The fourth task in planning the study answers the question, "Which participants will we include in the study's population?" The goal of this task is to set specific criteria for including individuals in the study. The criteria most often include job role and geographic location, and also the time span that has elapsed since these people have participated in the training being evaluated. Because the time frame is a major consideration in itself, it is discussed separately as the next consideration. The people who are defined as the population and the definition of the program go hand in hand. For instance, in the American Express example, we restricted the population to only regional executives, branch office managers, and financial advisors, as these were the principal target groups for the three variants of the training. Trainees who may have participated in one of the three variants, but who worked in other functions were not included, as they were not considered a critical population mass. For reasons of study logistics, we further limited the population to those participants who worked in the continental United States, as the programs provided to international audiences were considerably different in their structure. Further, there were only very few people included in the international programs.

This step also includes studying the participants within a single "program" to determine if there are subpopulations that we need to sample separately. The definition of subpopulations is necessary when some characteristic of the population is thought to affect the potential impact of the training. In our experience, we have found that organizational unit, geographic location, and years of experience in some related role are common (but not the only) characteristics that define subpopulations. For instance, in an evaluation of the implementation of an individual development planning system in a large oil company, it was necessary to carefully define both the population and subpopulations of employee to study. In a generic sense, the target population was all managers and all of their reporting employees. But senior human resources executives informed us that some of the refinery operations in New Jersey represented work cultures very different from those in corporate sales and support locations. Refineries were infamous for—and proud of —their roughhouse "dog eat dog" approach to work. If we were to combine data from these cultures with the milder and more human-relations sensitive environment in corporate offices, we would mislead ourselves as to how well and completely the system was being adopted.

Another typical way that we define subpopulations is by job role. In a management development program study, for example, we partitioned and sampled participants into production managers, sales and marketing managers, and managers in shared services functions (for example, corporate human resources). Readers should note that the definition of multiple populations might mean, for all intents and purposes, the subdivision of the SC study into several SC studies. This was definitely the case in the American Express Financial Advisors' study—we not only selected separate population samples, but also designed survey methods and interview protocols tailored to the needs of each population. Further, in developing the final conclusions, we were careful to document impact stories that represented each subpopulation. An important implication of the establishment of multiple populations is that they can very easily increase project costs: the study may require multiple surveys, multiple interview protocols, separate data analyses, and more time spent in identifying conclusions and recommendations.

5. How Soon After the Training to Conduct the Survey

The questions that we must answer here are, "What is the earliest that someone could have participated in this training to be part of the study population?" and "How recently can someone have participated in the training and still be included in the study?" When setting the early date, we have to consider whether the training has undergone a recent redesign; we would not want to go back beyond the implementation of the current design. In addition, there are practical issues to consider. We have found consistently that participants have difficulty remembering details of application and impact of training if their participation was over a year earlier.

Regarding the most recent inclusion date, we always try to determine how much time must have passed before someone could have reasonably applied the training and seen impact from these new behaviors. Consider two brief examples to illustrate this. In one study, we began the SCM effort on a Monday when the training had concluded the Friday of the week before. In this case, call center customer service reps had been trained to use a new call routing and response system that was intended to increase accuracy of responses to calls and decrease waiting time for customers. Clearly, the training was meant to be used immediately, and the cycle of impact was equally abrupt in that effects should be likewise immediately noticeable.

In the second example, sales reps in a business with a three-month sales cycle had received training in negotiation skills, hoping to achieve more favorable contract conditions. It was most likely that participants would need to wait for the right time and place to apply their learning, and this would vary over time for different participants. In this second case, we might wait two to three months to conduct a follow-up survey. The rule to follow is that we wait until there is a reasonable expectation for learning application and at least some resultant impact on key indicators of results, such as improvements in service, progress toward more sales, and so forth.

In some cases, such as with some forms of leadership and executive development, ultimate impact may be a long way off, perhaps even years. In these cases, it is important to define earlier indicators of learning application and interim progress toward more long term impact. It would not make sense to wait three years or more, as by then it is far too late to learn anything useful for subsequent waves of trainees, and conditions will have changed so much that it would be well nigh impossible to sort out impacts and outcomes due to the training. In virtually any training intervention, there must be some sort of behavioral change expected within a reasonably short period of time. If there is not, then we would have to inquire as to the integrity of the logic of the training. Why, if there is not an expectation for usage of the learning for a year would anyone be trained now?

6. Establishing a Schedule for the Study

We have to identify any time constraints on the study, especially the deadline by which the study must be complete, and also dates within the study that participants may not be available. It is not wise, for example, to distribute a survey just before a holiday period or to schedule interviews during a budget planning or frantic sales cycle.

One piece of advice here: be careful in making promises about time parameters. There are two aspects of a Success Case study that are notoriously difficult to manage. One is the time people will take in completing and returning a survey. The second aspect of the study that can take a long time is scheduling and completing Success Case interviews. However, these kinds of scheduling constraints are familiar to any investigator in an organizational setting. Common sense and application of good project management principles will enable timely and efficient completion of the study.

7. Specify and Confirm the Resources Available for the Study

A basic rule of any project planning effort must be to match the design to the available resources. If available resources are not sufficient to conduct the "ideal" Success Case evaluation for an initiative, practitioners can usually reframe the scope and design of the study so that they still obtain valuable and credible information.

Typically, the most expensive and time-consuming portions of a Success Case study are the survey, the interviews, and perhaps completing drafts of and getting reviews completed for a final report. Paper surveys require more effort and cost than electronic surveys. Readers are cautioned to carefully consider the survey process that will be used, and be sure it is within the budget available. In addition, the complexity of the sampling will affect the effort required, which in turn affects costs.

The interview portion of the study is typically the greatest cost determinant. While adding more respondents to an e-mail survey adds little effort or cost, increasing the number of interviews adds directly and proportionally to costs. As previously indicated, interviewing is time consuming, and almost always takes longer than expected, because of interrupted interviews, cancellations, false starts, and so forth. When estimating the number of interviews to conduct, the goal is to determine the fewest number of interviews to complete to yield the desired number of documented Success Cases and credible information about the overall impact of the training.

When budgeting for interviews, we typically estimate that it will take us three (3) hours of work to complete each 45-minute interview. This will include time for interview preparation (reviewing the interviewee's survey, for example), scheduling the call, conducting the interview, and reflecting on and writing up the notes afterwards. This three-hour estimate also includes a factor for cancellations and rescheduling, which always occurs with at least some interviews. Please note that this discussion applies only to telephone interviews, as opposed to face-to-face interviews, which are generally more time-intensive and expensive, especially if travel is necessary. With few exceptions, we successfully design most Success Case evaluations using telephone interviews.

8. Finalize the Success Case Strategy

This eighth decision point in the planning step requires synthesis of all the information gathered through all the planning steps to create a sound and feasible strategy for the specific study in question. There is no one single cookie-cutter design that works for all SCM efforts, though all share a common conceptual and process model. Each SCM practitioner needs to customize that framework to fit the needs, context, and resources of the client organization. We can, however, share some example strategies that we have used successfully in the past.

To this end, Table 4-1 presents a number of representative examples of Success Case studies we have conducted, each addressing a different evaluation purpose.

Table 4-1 Example Success Case Purposes and Strategies

The Client's Need and Purpose	The Success Case Strategy
Illustrating Impact A large telecommunications company had invested in a mandatory supervisor training program. Initial reports are that the program is popular, but the company wants some hard evidence about its impact. Senior managers are reluctant to send their people to something that doesn't pay off, especially as personnel shortages have stressed workloads.	Selected random samples of training participants from each major business unit and functional department, to be sure to represent all supervisors. Sent a survey to the samples, asking them to note which (from a list) supervisory actions they had tried and what beneficial results, if any, had been achieved. Documented successes in each of several major categories (for example, using the skills to avert a lawsuit, using the skills to increase production).
Illustrating Impact for "Marketing" A consulting firm that sells on-line coaching services to companies has had some initial successes. It wants to document these so that the "stories" of success can be used to market the service to other companies. The aim is to provide evidence to potential but skeptical buyers that this sort of service can really work.	Surveyed coaches to find out which of them reported the greatest success with their clients. Chose three success instances that represented the major categories of clients the firm worked with (high tech, manufacturing, healthcare) and documented these, showing especially the business results that clients had achieved as a result of the coaching services. *(continued)*

Table 4-1 Example Success Case Purposes and Strategies (Continued)

The Client's Need and Purpose	*The Success Case Strategy*
Determining How to Increase Impact A large computer company was receiving conflicting information about the effectiveness of a very expensive technical maintenance training course. Cost cutting pressures were very high, and the company had to determine quickly what about the program was working, and whether and how it could be improved.	Used a survey to identify extreme samples of successful applications of the training, and samples of those participants who were not using the training. While many users were very successful and achieved dramatic impact, a shocking proportion of participants were not using the training. By digging deep in follow-up interviews, we identified several key factors that the company could better manage (for example, trainee selection) to improve the proportion of successful trainees.
Determining Scope of Impact and "Unrealized" or Potential Impact A financial services company had invested a lot of money over the years in training its employees to use emotional intelligence skills. Anecdotal evidence showed that some parts of the organization were probably using the training a lot and getting good results, while others seemed to not be using the training very much. The training department needed to decide (a) whether the training could be revised to get greater impact for more people, and (b) what concrete steps could be taken to assure more impact.	Collected representative Success Case examples from extreme groups of people getting a great deal of value, and no value at all. An analysis of workplace factors that were consistently related to differences in impact led to suggestions for changing the training, and for changing how supervisors managed access and application of the training. These changes, it was estimated, could more than double the scope and value of the training's impact.

Chapter Five

Constructing a Simple Training Impact Model

*P*robably all readers, either as a child or perhaps as a parent, have
been on a long family automobile trip when, from the backseat,
comes the infamous and recurring question, "Are we there yet?" The
word "there," of course, stands for the destination of the trip. In reference to
the Success Case Method, the destination of the training's trip is the business
results the training is intended to achieve. The route to this business impact is
through the on-the-job application of learning that we hope participants will
make as a result of their training. That is, the training is successful when trainees use their learning in key on-job application behaviors, and these then help
them produce results that benefit the business. With a clear understanding
of the intended outcomes, behaviors, and skills of a training program—the
"route" to impact—we have the information we need to build the SCM survey
and interview tools needed to conduct an SCM study..

The Success Case Method defines "success" very clearly: the achievement
of a positive impact on the organization through the application of some skill

or knowledge acquired in training. As we saw in the previous chapter, one of the early and critical tasks is to clearly define and document the intended impact of the training, so that the evaluators can measure the actual impact against the intended organizational outcomes of the training. The tool that we use to capture the intended impact of training is called an "impact model."

Figure 5-1 shows a simple though typical impact model for a training program in which hotel housekeepers had been trained as part of a larger customer service quality improvement effort.

Knowledge + Skills	Critical Actions	Key Results	Business Unit Goals (Guest Services)	Hotel Company Goals
Able to use appropriate cleaning equipment and supplies	Clean and prepare guest rooms Recognize needs for cleaning services and take appropriate action	All rooms fully cleaned for occupancy with no discrepancies	Complete guest satisfaction	A fully satisfying guest experience for each hotel
Knowledge of hotel locations and services Guest relations skills	Respond completely and accurately to guest questions	Guests requests for service fulfilled completely, accurately, and on time	All guest areas spotlessly clean, safe and fully stocked with amenities	Increase return business rate an average of 20% across all guest categories
Knowledge of hotel standards for safe and fully equipped guest areas	Provide additional services on request of guests and assure guest satisfaction with response Provide emergency cleaning services as needed and on request	Complete satisfaction of guests requests Emergency needs met		

Figure 5-1 Impact Model for Hotel Housekeeping Staff

This impact model (Figure 5-1) shows information in several categories such as the following:

- The knowledge and skill outcomes that trainees (hotel housekeepers) were intended to master in the training program.
- The major ways in which these learning outcomes were to be applied in the housekeepers' job behaviors.
- The results that theses job applications were intended to produce.
- The business goals (unit and company level) to which this learning was meant to contribute.

The hotel was providing the housekeeper training as part of a larger initiative to increase the satisfaction of hotel guests that in turn was part of a business strategy to increase the return business rate, a common business metric for the hotel business, as it is more profitable to retain people as regular hotel guests than it is to attract new guests.

It is important to note that this impact model is used to guide the initial inquiry, and it does not mean that a training program is absolutely successful if it achieves the intended outcomes it aimed for. It is possible, for instance, that a program might achieve its intended outcomes but at the same time lead to unintended outcomes that detract from or even outweigh the value of the intended results. Or, a program might achieve its intended outcomes but at a cost that is far too high and thus cannot be considered to be valuable since its costs outweigh its benefits. Later in the book we address these issues and provide guidance for how the thoughtful SCM practitioner can assess unintended outcomes and balance these against the outcomes the program aimed for.

Elements of the Impact Model

The purpose of the model is to depict the ideal or intended impact of training, as well as the individual results, behaviors, and capabilities that are needed to achieve that impact. Otherwise put, an impact model provides the answers to these questions, which are clarified below:

- To what organizational goals would the training contribute?
- What trainee job results would it help achieve?
- What different/improved behaviors would the trainee demonstrate on the job as a result of training?
- What new or improved capabilities would the trainee acquire?

To What Organizational Goals Would the Training Contribute?

The organizational goal to which a training program is linked may be an overall organizational goal, or it may be the goal of a smaller organizational unit. This will depend on the nature and scope of the program for which you are planning a SCM study. An evaluation of emotional intelligence training at American Express Financial Advisors, for example, was an organization-wide initiative that involved many people in a number of roles. In this case, the program was intended to help achieve the organization's overall goals of maintaining and expanding the customer base, increasing sales, and retaining employees (especially advisors)—and the impact model included those organization-wide goals. In another case, however, the focus of the evaluation may be on one unit or division within the organization. This was the case with the hotel guest services evaluation that was the basis for the impact model in Figure 5-1. In these instances, the entries in the farthest right-hand column may represent only work unit objectives (or both work-unit and organizational objectives).

The reason we include this column in an impact model is to be sure that we have understood the organizational value to which the training is intended to contribute, and that our client agrees with our understanding. As we finalize the SCM study, we will want to make conclusions about the impact and value of the training initiative that we have evaluated, and thus this understanding up front as to the ultimate goals of the training is vital.

What Trainee Job Results Would the Training Help Achieve?

Trainees are typically individual performers or teams whose actions have an immediate result for which they are accountable. We need to identify the intended job-level results as these might be vital in designing the survey portion of the SCM study in order to sort out and differentiate highly successful candidates from those less successful cases. We will also need to know what sorts of results to look for in the interview phase of the study. And finally, simply asking the question about immediate job results and their relationship to final business goals promotes a worthwhile dialogue with the client and assures that we understand the rationale for and intended impact of the training.

What Different/Improved Behaviors Would the Trainee Demonstrate on the Job as a Result of Training?

A significant portion of the Success Case data collection process, in both the survey and interview phases, revolves around identifying what the trainee actually did after training that led to positive results. Specifically, the study team needs to learn what new behaviors were performed because the trainee acquired new skills and knowledge in the training. It is important to remember, however, that training initiatives only build capability—they give participants the skills and knowledge they need to do something new. The trainee must convert the capability into performance to produce valuable results. A task of the study team is to learn what the trainee did differently, if anything, because of the training.

In order for the evaluators to probe effectively for this information, the impact model must present the specific behaviors the training was intended to make possible. During the SCM inquiry, of course, we may probe for and discover many applications of learning beyond what we listed on the impact model. This is well and good, and in fact is an aim of any SCM effort. But, to know where to begin to look and what to search for, the initial impact model is an indispensable guide.

What New or Improved Capabilities Would the Trainee Acquire?

Though trainee performance is actually the focus of a SCM study, the success model always includes the definition of the capabilities that training is intended to build. Evaluators at times find that a lack of broad impact was due to a failure of the training to produce the desired capability—in sum, the learning-to-performance chain broke during the learning event itself. Including intended capabilities on the impact model allows the evaluators to knowledgeably study this link in the chain.

In summary, the impact model guides the entire SCM process. Once intended outcomes are sufficiently clear and there is a sufficient level of agreement to proceed, the impact model serves as the basis for the survey. Since the goal of the survey process is to discover those participants who report the greatest (and least) application of their learning, it is necessary to know what success would look like, so that the survey items will effectively screen for the extremes of this success. The impact model also guides the interview portion of the study. Success Case method interviews are intended to describe and document successful applications in detail. Understanding what the training set out to accomplish enables interviewers to focus their questions carefully in order to determine to what extent training has really led to worthwhile actions and results.

Because a thorough SCM study must investigate unintended consequences of training, the impact model does not limit inquiry, but serves to provide an initial focus. If we know, for example, that the training was intended to promote more dialogue between sales reps and customers to determine needs more accurately, this may help us also to look for possible negative outcomes, such as sales reps spending too much time on accounts where dialogue is easily established and avoiding accounts where analyses of true customer needs may be more difficult.

Constructing an Impact Model

The construction of an impact model is a relatively simple process, once the planning process has been completed. It is mostly a process of asking questions and otherwise gathering information about the training to be evaluated, and trying out successive drafts and iterations of an impact model until clarity and agreement are reached. Often we will begin asking questions about the training to be evaluated as we are first meeting with stakeholders in the very first contact with a potential SCM client. Beyond that, sources of information to complete the model depend on the nature of the information sought.

Table 5-1 provides some suggestions and guidance for gathering data for each of the impact model information categories, and will serve as a useful guide for readers.

Table 5-1 Suggestions for Gathering Impact Model Data

Impact Model Category	Suggestions
Business Goals	• Determine the highest level goal that should be identified to justify and demonstrate the worth of the program (for example, overall organization goal? Division goal? Work unit goal? More than one level of goal?) • Interview program designers and/or leaders • Ask questions of any available stakeholders • Talk with senior executives and leaders • Analyze business plans or strategic white-papers • Read annual reports • Review the company's website

(continued)

Table 5-1 Suggestions for Gathering Impact Model Data (Continued)

Impact Model Category	Suggestions
Key Results (intended job/team application outcomes)	• Review performance appraisal instruments, job descriptions • Interview a few managers of program participants • Analyze the program learning objectives and extrapolate job applications from these • Review program case studies and examples • Interview program designers and/or leaders • Visit some job sites and ask questions • Interview a few available program participants
Critical Actions (intended behavioral applications of the program capabilities)	• Analyze the program objectives • Review program case studies and examples • Interview program designers and/or leaders • Visit with and interview a few available program participants and/or their managers • Review job descriptions, job models, competency models
Program Capabilities (the skills and knowledge that the training targets)	• Observe the program in action (for example, sit in on a training session) • Review program materials • Interview program designers and/or leaders

The authors provide these suggestions for writing effective impact model items:

• Structure all items in a column the same way. For example, skills and knowledge might always use the prefix "ability to . . ." Or, job results can be written as past-tense outcomes, for example, "accurate records completed."

- Word the goal statements as they are worded in the organization's documentation or stated by the stakeholders

- Word the job results as accomplished outcomes, such as "a 5% increase in sales," as opposed to "increase sales by 5%," which reads more like a behavior than an outcome

- Begin behaviors with a verb, such as "Identify emerging conflicts using the Conflicts Checklist." Be sure they are specific. Also be sure they are the most high-leverage and vital job application behaviors needed to contribute to business impact.

The last step in creating the impact model is to validate it. This is especially important when model data has been collected from a number of stakeholders at different times or in different locations. The consequences of not gaining stakeholder buy-in to the finished model before the study is begun are quite simply that the study could be useless to the organization. Since the impact model is the guide for data collection, analysis, and reporting, errors on the model may lead to collecting data on the wrong skills, behaviors, results, and/or goals.

How Many Impact Models Are Needed?

The number of impact models to be developed for a SCM study is dependent on the number of different roles that are the target audiences for the training. For example, in an evaluation of sales training for sales representatives in different sales divisions, the behaviors and job results were mostly very similar even though the products sold and the markets to whom they were sold differed widely. But, because the sales process was the same—in fact, a replicable and standardized sales process was the purpose for the training in the first place—the same impact model was sufficient to guide inquiry across all sales roles. In another case, customer service skills training in automobile dealerships, the skills taught were all the same. But, the ways in which the skills would be used in the workplace differed by the role of the trainees. Service writers, salespeople, financial officers, and receptionists would all have different tasks into which they would incorporate the skills taught. Thus, we prepared a separate impact model for each of these roles.

How Much Specificity Is Required?

There have been several instances where we were unable to define an impact model with much specificity because the training program leaders were very uncertain about how the training might be applied. A large grant-making foundation, for example, invested considerable efforts in providing training in systems thinking for almost all of its staff members. This effort was driven by a perceived need to promote more cross-functional communications and to break down "silos" in the organization that seemed to limit interaction among staff members located in different parts of the organization. There was a feeling among the leadership as well that the workplace culture was resistant to sharing of information and as a result best practices were not being shared or leveraged. Beyond this, the training leaders were not able to define any organizational impacts that were previously defined as goals other than that senior leaders hoped to create an organizational culture that was more characteristic of a "learning organization." In this case, the impact model was very vague, though this did not impede the conduct of the SCM study.

Lacking a clear and specific impact model, we proceeded by identifying the major job roles that were involved in the training. From there, we designed a survey that simply asked respondents to report whether they had been able to use their recent training in any way that they believed had led to an important result that the foundation would value. This survey yielded a relatively large number of success "claims" that we then had to pursue in depth during the interview portion of the study. Eventually, after many interviews and many false-positive interviews, we isolated and described several major impacts of the training that were recognized as valuable and worthy by the program owners and their senior leaders. But, this took more time and energy than it would have had we been able to define a more detailed impact model from the beginning.

In situations like this, where there has been considerable investment in training but no one is quite sure specifically what value the training should have led to or if it has led to any value at all, the SCM study becomes a sort of "fishing expedition" where we look broadly for valuable outcomes, and the impact model becomes a final product of the SCM process, not something we produce in detail beforehand.

It is useful to note here that, to some extent, all SCM studies are still fishing expeditions of a sort regardless of how firmly and specifically a client is able to help us formulate an impact model beforehand. That is, the purpose of the SCM evaluation is to search out and discover the real and actualized value of a training program if there is any. This may be exactly the same value the program designers and sponsors intended, or it may be different in some ways from the aimed-for goals. Thus, an impact model is always a final product of a SCM study, though in this case, it is a model that shows the key ways that program's trainees actually used their training and the actual results and value, if any, that these applications of learning led to.

In summary, some Success Case studies will require you to complete a fairly detailed and precise impact model at the beginning of the study, so that you understand how the program was intended to work and then focus your inquiry on highly specific and precise actions and results. In other cases, you may begin the study with only a rudimentary and sketchy impact model. How much of an impact model you need at the front end of the study will be driven by the purpose for the study and the information needs of key stakeholders.

The impact model is a powerful tool for concisely depicting the chain of events from training to organizational impact. Stakeholders value these models for their clarity and intuitively understand that there can be many other applications for the models. For the evaluation team, however, the impact model is the spine around which the body of the evaluation is built. The next step in this process is to design and develop the survey, which is discussed in Chapter Six.

Fishing for Success— Conducting the SCM Survey

*T*he Success Case Method survey has two major objectives: to identify those training participants who have experienced the greatest and the least success in applying their learning, and to gain an estimate of the scope of success for the entire training population. The survey is analogous to a net that we cast into the sea of past training participants in order to hoist up the best samples we can catch of those participants most likely to have used their training to achieve worthwhile results, and those at the opposite end of the learning application spectrum, those least likely to have used their training successfully. Once we have culled the most and the least likely success candidates (the biggest and the smallest fish, so to speak), we will investigate their experiences in depth to determine exactly how successful, or unsuccessful, each of them has in fact been, and the factors that explain their success or the lack of it.

The survey net we cast is also meant to give us an estimate of the proportion of successful users of training and the proportion of less-than-successful users of training. Putting these information elements together with the in-depth data from the interview phase of the study lets us make reliable estimates of the overall success of a training venture, explaining and documenting the value it produces when it is used, how often and broadly it is used successfully, and the value it could have produced had it been used by more trainees in more successful applications.

In this chapter, we explain in greater detail exactly how to plan, design, administer, and analyze SCM surveys. We begin with an explanation of the general nature of a SCM survey, then proceed to explain the steps involved in planning and survey design, providing several examples of SCM survey formats. In the latter portion of the chapter, we explain how survey data are analyzed to pinpoint the most and least likely success candidates. We also discuss the process for analyzing survey data to make estimates of the range and scope of impact.

Defining the Survey Step

We need to have a way to sort through each and every person in our defined training population and determine which small groups of these to interview. This "sorting" is the survey step. By the end of this step, we want to know who applied something learned in training with the greatest impact, and who did not apply learning, or who tried to apply learning but saw no worthwhile impact or otherwise abandoned their efforts to use their training.

Usually, a formal survey is the best method to use. We rarely use a paper survey any more unless the pool of training graduates cannot be reached by e-mail or is otherwise inaccessible via electronic technologies. The additional advantage of a survey is that it provides some further quantitative information about the nature and scope of the success. That is, after a survey, we may be able to conclude that, for instance, "63% of all the sales representatives who attended laptop training applied at least one of the six key behaviors taught in the class."

We have conducted several SCM evaluation studies where we have not used a formal survey. Instead, we have gone directly to data or information sources that can guide us to the most probable successful users of training and those probable least successful users. In an evaluation of some sales training, for example, we analyzed sales performance data for the calendar quarter following the training program and identified those sales reps that had most increased their sales performance, and those sales reps that had the least success in sales performance. Then, we interviewed a sample of these most and least successful sales reps to determine what, if any, role their training had played in their success.

Not using a formal survey has the advantage of getting to possible Success Cases quickly. It also may eliminate possible biases deriving from self-report methods, as actual performance data can be used to locate potential training successes. But not using a survey of all trainees obviates being able to estimate the range or scope of training impact. For this reason, we almost always use surveys in conducting SCM studies.

Conducting the SCM Survey

The basic steps of designing and implementing a SCM survey are as follows:

1. Determine the survey population.
2. Plan the survey access, distribution, and return process (for example, e-mail, web, mailed letters).
3. Determine the nature and scope of data the survey must gather.
4. Construct the survey items, using the impact model as a reference.
5. Identify a scoring scheme.
6. Distribute and follow up on the survey.

Each of these steps is discussed in more detail in the remainder of this chapter.

Step One: Identify the Survey Recipients

A fundamental step in the survey planning process is deciding which training graduates to include in and define as the "population" of trainees to be included in the SCM survey. The definition of the trainee population is driven by two basic questions:

What types of personnel completed the program?

When did they complete the training?

The Types of Trainees Involved   Imagine, for example, that 700 managers had completed a training program that we wish to evaluate. Among these 700 are managers in the areas of sales, factory operations, personnel, quality control, corporate services, and branch operations. Here we have managers from six (6) different functions in the organization. If it is likely that this training would have had different sorts of impact and valuable outcomes depending on the function in which these managers worked, then it may be important to treat each category of manager as a separate trainee population. In this case, it might be necessary to construct six (6) different survey formats, each with different sorts of items depending on the nature of impact to be expected. At this point, the reader is encouraged to re-visit the impact models described in the previous chapter. If these impact models indeed make it clear that the nature of impact will vary according to organizational unit, then it may be advisable to consider a separate survey format for each of the six (6) groups. Imagine, for example, that the principal business issue in quality is retention of workers, and thus it was hoped that quality managers would use their training to become more effective in personnel supervision so that they would help retain and develop successful performers. On the other hand, imagine that the principal business issue in factory operations was increasing productivity and reducing scrap. In this part of the company, we would hope that managers would use their training to provide better direction, coaching, and feedback to improve performance. In this case, it might be best to construct different survey formats and deal with each subcategory of manager as a separate population.

Another solution to this issue of differential types of impact would be to construct a more general survey format that contained items inclusive of all types of training applications and outcomes, then sorting respondents into groups according to their organizational category so that Success and non-Success Cases could be pursued in each of these different categories during the interview phase of the SCM study.

Here, there is a trade-off between reliability and accuracy and efficiency. It would be more efficient to use a single survey format with more general items. But, such an approach could have a negative impact on the accuracy of the survey, because the items would necessarily have to be more general and thus less specific. If the nature of impact expected is quite substantially different, and if it is quite important to know how well the training is working across the different organizational units, then we would advise separate survey formats for each trainee group, as this will produce more accurate data and make it easier to definitively pinpoint likely Success Cases in each trainee category. On the other hand, if the nature of expected impact does not vary markedly, then a single survey would work, and we would simply identify and select for interview success candidates in each of the several trainee category types.

When Was Training Completed?   We are always asked this question in SCM training workshops and presentations: "How soon after the training do you follow up the trainees; six weeks, three months, six months?" Like the answer to all important questions, the answer to this one is: "It depends." But the variable on which the answer depends is quite straightforward and clear. How long after the training you conduct the survey depends on how long it would take for someone to make a reasonably effective application of their training. In one SCM study, we were evaluating the impact of training for customer service representatives who worked in a call center. The purpose of the training was to give them skills in asking better questions at the beginning of a call so that they could make appropriate use of new software that would let them access data more quickly and thoroughly respond to customer concerns. In this case, the training was delivered on a Friday and we conducted the survey the following Monday. Why so fast? We followed up so quickly because this training should have been put to use immediately after the training. If it was not used then, chances that it would ever be used correctly would decline. Further, the client needed to locate and document how well the training was being used so that this information could be leveraged into improving the training and its application for subsequent groups of trainees.

In another case, we waited 12 months after the training. This instance involved training for purchasing agents to help them negotiate and close supplier agreements that were more strategic and cost-effective. The typical negotiation and agreement closing cycle was several months in duration, and it would not be important to use it in every single agreement, only those that were of a sufficient size to make the most business sense. Thus, 12 months was needed to be sure that these trainees had sufficient time to apply their training and that we could tap into a sufficient number and range of training applications.

In either case, it is important not to allow your SCM survey to extend too far back into time, because if too much time has passed since the training, it is more likely that memory will fade and become confused with other training and development interventions.

Do You Need to Survey Everyone? In most cases, we include all of the defined population (for example, all 300 sales managers who completed a training course between May and November) in the survey. Given the extremely low costs of electronic survey methods and the fact that SCM surveys are typically very brief and take respondents less than three minutes or so to complete, there is little to be gained from drawing samples for the survey.

Step Two: Plan the Survey Access, Distribution, and Return Process

Today there are a number of media that can be used to convey the survey items to participants. On occasion, we use the hard-copy written and mailed survey, but only when conditions prohibit the use of internet technology. Clearly, hard-copy surveys are more expensive since they involve postage and printing costs. Even so, there may be times when a mailed hard-copy survey is desirable. In one case, for example, we needed to survey a small group (less than 50) of senior-level executives. As these people tended to be older in age and very busy people, we feared that an e-mail approach might get lost in the morass of similar messages. Thus, we chose to use a hard-copy survey form that we sent to each respondent using a commercial express mail vendor. While this was costly (costing $12.00 per person for mailing expenses), we felt that the express mail service would make the survey more noticeable and would also convey its importance. This was, however, a rare circumstance.

We have also, on occasion, used a live telephone survey where we posed the survey questions in a one-on-one conversation with each participant in the survey sample. Again, this was an unusual circumstance with a very small population, and it enabled us to collect data in one step, and if the respondent was clearly a strong success, we continued straight into an in-depth interview.

In almost all cases today, we distribute surveys electronically via e-mail, or send an e-mail message to solicit participation, providing a web-address for the survey itself. Web-based survey applications are especially effective and efficient, as they come with a broad array of features that save time and effort. In sum, the basic rule for selecting a survey medium is to choose the medium that, first, allows the greatest number of participants to respond; and second, allows for survey creation, distribution, and data analysis and is as cost- and time- effective as possible.

Soliciting Participation   In all SCM applications, there is a need to solicit participation from the population to be surveyed. That is, someone needs to inform them about the purposes for the SCM survey and ask them to participate. This is usually accomplished with a cover letter or cover e-mail that is sent to everyone in the selected population, with the cover letter signed by an influential leader—preferably, the most influential person that one can get to agree to serve in this capacity. Increasingly, people in organizations are plagued by many requests to participate in surveys, and so it is necessary to give them a good reason to get involved. Thus, it helps when potential respondents receive a request from someone in a position of authority.

One must be careful, however, to assure that the cover letter will not introduce a bias into the responses by giving the perception that there is an expectation for a positive (or negative) reaction. The cover letter should be neutral in tone, expressing only that participation is important, but that all points of view are welcome and important.

Step Three: Determine the Nature and Scope of Data the Survey Must Gather

As we noted earlier in the chapter, the goal that the Success Case survey must achieve is to identify the trainees with the greatest likelihood of having high success or non-success stories to share. In some surveys, this is the only purpose we attempt to achieve. This type of single-purpose survey is usually very brief, as it has only to gather sufficient information to discriminate the high-success and low-success trainees from the remainder of the population.

In most cases, you will want to be able to gauge and report the extent to which training was applied in each of several separate and distinct application categories. In an evaluation of laptop computer usage among sales reps, for instance, we wanted to know whether the laptops had been used to analyze accounts, prepare presentations, track account performance, plan schedules, and so forth. Some of these applications of the laptop capability were considered to be highly strategic, and were the principal hoped-for outcome, while other applications were less strategic, such as using the technology to maintain a calendar and prepare graphics for a presentation. Thus, we were careful to include items in the survey that would assess application in each of the several categories.

There may be a need in some surveys to include items that assess demographic variables, such as how long a person has been in a particular job role, or in what division they work. Most often, however, since the SCM survey is not anonymous, it is easy to capture such demographic data elsewhere, and not have to add length to the survey with demographic items. To keep overall response rates as high as possible, our goal for a SCM survey is that it should contain only about six to ten items at the most, and it should take a typical respondent no more than three to four minutes to complete.

Despite the fact that the typical SCM survey is short, its responses can nevertheless be aggregated and analyzed to provide a quantitative estimate of the nature and scope of impact. We could report, for instance, that "Of the survey respondents, 8% reported using the laptop to analyze an existing account and prepare a revenue increasing strategy." Another finding from the survey might be, "The most common application of the laptop (63% of respondents) was to schedule appointments while only 8% of respondents reported using the laptop to identify revenue enhancement opportunities."

Whenever we can, we avoid adding length to the SCM survey, trying to get additional data, if it is truly needed, from other sources. We also resist adding any items to the survey that focus on other training variables or conditions, such as whether participants enjoyed the training, or what parts of the training they felt were most effective. Again, an SCM study has a tightly focused purpose, and we work very hard to keep the survey as short and sharply targeted as it can be.

Step Four: Construct the Survey Items, Using the Impact Model as a Reference

As noted, the SCM survey is usually very short and tightly focused on the key behaviors that would be carried out by participants if the training is being used successfully. These behaviors should already have been defined to a great extent in the impact model discussed in the previous chapter.

SCM survey items often have a two-part structure as follows:

1. The extent of several applications of one or more of the training outcomes, and

2. The extent to which the behavior led to a positive outcome

Figure 6-1 shows the content of a typical SCM survey in its entirety. Of course, this content may be formatted differently as needed to fit an electronic template, as used in a web-based survey. But the items and response choices are exactly as shown in Figure 6-1

Introduction

This survey asks six questions about the Performance Management workshop that you recently attended. While we will ask you about your actions since the training, this is not an evaluation of you or anyone else. The sole purpose is to assess the effectiveness and quality of the training.

Your responses are confidential. No individual comments or data will be shared with anyone at XYZ Company. The survey asks for your name only because the evaluation consultants may wish to telephone some respondents to get more information.

To respond to the survey, click on the response choice that best reflects your experience. When you have completed each item and added your name, click on "Submit" to complete the survey process. The survey should take approximately three minutes to complete.

Thank you! We appreciate your honest and helpful feedback.

Your Company President

Figure 6-1 Typical SCM Survey

I. Here are some actions you may have taken since the Performance Management training. Please check the response opposite each action that best reflects your experience since participating in the training.

Possible Action: Used the Perform- ance Management Principles training to . . .	1. Tried this and achieved a concrete and worthwhile result	2. Tried this, but have not noticed any results	3. Tried this, but it did not work	4. Have not tried this yet
Set and communicated expectations for my team				

(continued)

Possible Action: Used the Perform-ance Management Principles training to . . .	1. Tried this and achieved a concrete and worthwhile result	2. Tried this, but have not noticed any results	3. Tried this, but it did not work	4. Have not tried this yet
Provided coaching to help improve performance				
Diagnosed perfor-mance problems				
Helped a team solve a performance problem				

2.	Which statement below best describes your experience since participating in the Performance Management training?

a. I learned something new, I have used it, and it has led to some very worthwhile results.

b. I learned and tried some new things but can't point to any very worthwhile results yet.

c. While I may have learned something new, I have not been able to use it yet.

d. I already knew about and was doing the things this training taught.

e. I don't think I can really use what I learned in the training.

3.	Name: _____

Your name is needed only because our evaluation consultants may want to follow up with some respondents. Data collected will be held in strictest confidence. Individual responses will not be shared within XYZ.

Notice that the survey consists of two principal items: which actions were taken and the extent to which these actions led to results, and an overall summary item that expresses the extent to which the training was used to achieve results. This is a very common SCM survey structure. The first item allows us to estimate the nature and scope of training application across several types of learning applications. Responses to this sort of item are useful to assess how trainees used their learning, and of course they also enable us to determine categories of probable success for later sampling. The second item gives an estimate of the extent to which, in general, the learning has produced impact. This is to some extent redundant of the first question, but this is intentional. First, this second item picks up any unanticipated applications of learning not found on the list in the first item. Second, the combined responses to both items one and two give us a more reliable indication of claimed impact. Both of these are, of course, self reports, and carry with them the usual sorts of threats to validity that any self reports engender. This is not a big concern, however, as the interview portion of the SCM process not only documents Success Cases, but serves to validate survey response trends. We can establish a probable "false positive" rate by simply calculating the proportion of true successes that we find among the group of claimed successes. We can do the same sort of analysis with any other success category, thus enabling quite reliable and valid conclusions about the actual impact of the training.

Here are some further issues to keep in mind when wording survey items:

- The wording in the highest success-level item response choice should be rigorous and exclusive, as you do not want to exacerbate a possible false-positive response rate. False positives drive up your costs, as they make it necessary for you to interview increasingly more highest-response category respondents to find a true success.

- Use items that express clear and definitive behaviors, so that you exclude respondents that may have merely enjoyed the training, or found that it was probably useful, but in fact have not really used it to accomplish a result.

- Provide response choices that allow for enough range of possible application outcomes, such as the person who has tried out the training and believes it is working, but can't claim any observable or concrete results. You may need to go searching for possible success cases among this second, less certain response category.

- Provide for a reasonable range of response that includes some fairly negative outcomes. Be careful not to bias the survey toward the positive end by not allowing for such negative responses.

- Be honest and forthright, allowing respondents to likewise choose a category that fits their experience and does not force them to "sugar coat" or otherwise provide a misleading response.

- Give people a socially acceptable and face-saving way to tell you that they really did not get any impact from the training, such as, "I have not yet had an opportunity to apply my training."

- Ask for the name of the respondent. This is necessary in the SCM survey as we need to identify individual responses by name so that we can, if we choose, follow up with an interview.

Step Five: Identify a Scoring Scheme

In this step, you determine how you would score the returned instruments and how you would determine what sorts of responses constitute a success or lack of success. You may redefine this scheme once you review actual responses, as these should guide you in the final determination of which respondents to include in the several success categories.

In the survey shown in Figure 6-1, we would define a clear high success as a respondent that made choice number one (". . . achieved a concrete and worthwhile result") for any learning applications in the first item, and also gave response choice (a) in the second item. Note that we do not assume that a person is more successful if they used the learning in more ways. Using learning in only one way, if it helps to achieve a positive outcome, is certainly deemed a success. In many cases, the people who use their training in only one application achieve more substantial results than those who apply their learning in a large number of ways.

Non-successes were defined as anyone who responded with no number one choices in the first item, and response choice c, d, or e to the second item.

Respondents who chose choice number two in each training application category in the first item (that is, no responses for number one in the first item) and choice b in the second item were considered a possible high success or probable low success. A sample from this pool of respondents would need to be interviewed to decide whether this group is really a positive success, and perhaps responded modestly, or that they were really non-successes, and had perhaps responded a bit ambitiously. We would know from the interviews what proportion of this group to ascribe to the high-success category, and what proportion to ascribe to the non-success category. Without a follow up interview, there is really no way to interpret this response group.

A final group of response scores could be deemed as "wafflers", or otherwise indeterminate. These are people that responded in a contradictory manner, either checking some number one choices in the first item, but then choosing something other than response a in the second item, or choosing response a in the second item, but not selecting any number one choices from the first item. Again, it takes a phone call to determine what has really gone on with respondents in this contradictory pattern response group. Another choice one has is to simply remove these respondents from the data set. But where there are a large number of such contradictory respondents, we usually telephone a random sample of them to find out how to interpret the responses.

Providing Enough Rigor and Spread   An important consideration for practitioners is to make sure that the survey scoring scheme is not too "easy" (or too hard). That is, success should not be defined so laxly that

virtually all respondents qualify as high successes. While it is possible
that everyone has indeed been successful, experience says that this is
not likely. In the rare instances where the program has in fact worked so
well that huge numbers have been successful, the evaluation team needs
to be sure that this high reporting of success is based on a sufficiently
rigorous definition. On the other hand, success should not be defined
so rigorously that no one could have possibly achieved it. The key here
is to provide enough response choices, across a wide range of possible
outcome scenarios. This will assure that the survey has enough spread in
all scores to identify the relatively small extreme groups to interview in
depth.

Step Six: Distribute and Follow Up On the Survey

The most complex elements of the survey process are complete at this
point. What remains is to format the survey in the selected medium
and take whatever steps are necessary to prepare it for distribution.
For paper-based surveys, this includes printing the survey copies,
preparing a cover letter and return envelopes (with postage), collating
the documents, stuffing the outgoing envelopes, affixing postage, and
mailing. For web and e-mail surveys, the items need to be formatted in
the survey application, an e-mail cover message needs to be created, the
survey needs to be posted to the web or included in the e-mail, and e-
mail addresses need to be compiled.

Final survey formats should be reviewed by stakeholders for approval. In some cases, approval will be needed from a company's legal
department. With web-based surveys, it is also wise to conduct a trial of
the survey to be sure that respondents can get through any firewalls or
other electronic barriers that may interfere with responding or collating
responses.

Once the preparation for distribution is complete, the surveys can be
distributed. It is important that the cover letter or message accompanying
the survey specify a return-by date, although the study team typically has

no means of enforcing that date. One strategy the authors use to promote response is to have an executive sponsor of the study send a message in advance of the survey stressing the importance of responding. This executive message has been very effective.

The team must now wait for responses to arrive. About mid-way through the survey response period, the evaluators should send out a follow-up letter or message to non-respondents. The follow-up process is not complex; it consists of sending a brief follow-up message encouraging participants to respond to the survey. For electronic surveys, the message might include the survey or hyperlink to the Web again. It is usually not feasible to re-send paper-based surveys, but we have found it effective to include a phone number and to offer to fax another survey to anyone who calls us with this request.

In most studies, a single follow-up is sufficient. When a survey yields a lower than expected response rate, we may consider additional follow-up actions (for example, asking the executive sponsor to send another message). The critical balance to achieve here is to encourage response without giving the appearance of harassing recipients, which is certain to discourage response.

Sorting the "Catch"— Analyzing Survey Results

*I*n the preceding chapter, we explored the process for surveying the training population to identify potential high- and low-success cases to interview and to gauge the nature and scope of training effects. In Chapter Seven we focus on the process of analyzing and scoring the "catch" of survey responses. The analysis that is conducted typically has two purposes: first and foremost, to identify the respondents with whom we will conduct follow-up interviews; and second, to develop estimates of the range, nature, and scope of application of training across the entire training population.

Scoring and Sorting the Survey Response

First we need, systematically and objectively, to sort the participants into three groups: high successes, low successes, and the "in-betweens" who likely experienced some, but limited, positive impacts from the training. Once the sorting is complete, the next step is to select the interviewees from among the high and low success candidates, and perhaps from the middle categories.

The initial projected scoring scheme now has to be revisited in light of the actual survey response patterns. We might have set an initially projected very high cut-off score for what we assumed would be our highest category of success, but find from the response pattern that very few if any respondents landed in that category. Now it is incumbent on us to conduct interviews from the highest score group that we did achieve, and find out what the actual nature of their experience was, and whether it still represents some worthwhile level of positive impact. Or, on the other hand, we may find that no one responded in the lowest category, and thus we will have to explore via interviews the next-to-lowest category to find out if this group represents truly low impact, or if perhaps they are a group that has indeed achieved worthy results.

We typically use a simple sorting process. For paper or telephone surveys, we simply review each completed survey and sort them into piles according to the level of response. We might, for example, create four piles of surveys: clearly strong positives, somewhat strong positives, moderate or indeterminate success, and low or no success. The number and nature of these piles will vary according to the actual survey response. There might be more or less piles depending on the overall response pattern. After all the piles are formed, we label each pile and then write the participant's success category (for example, "strong positive") on the survey instrument.

Even when we have used a Web-based or other electronic medium, we still very often print out all of the surveys and sort them into piles. While it is labor intensive to print copies of the surveys, it is also helpful, as we will want to have the physical survey copy in hand for each respondent that we decide to interview. For electronic surveys where we have a large number of responses, say several hundred, we would rely on a summary calculation from the survey database collating all the scores into a spreadsheet or other format where each line on the document represents one participant's responses to all of the items. Most survey applications allow the data to be imported into other databases or spreadsheet formats. Then the evaluation team can set up the spreadsheet to calculate, record, and rank the scores right in the spreadsheet. This electronic scoring and sorting is both convenient and time-efficient, as the team is not dependent on having to manually shuffle through large stacks of survey documents; the data and scores are displayed together on just a few pages.

We usually estimate that only one out of every two interviews will actually result in a reportable story—therefore, the candidate pool should be at least twice the number of final cases to be documented. If fewer than three of the initial six turn out to be valid Success Cases worthy of documentation, we make note of this so that we are reliably estimating our false-positive rate, then return to the survey results and choose a few more of the highest-scoring respondents to continue the search for the best success stories.

Of course, we also search among the very lowest scoring candidates to develop an understanding of the factors and characteristics that seem to influence a lack of impact. Thus, we repeat the sort of scoring process we use for high successes with the lowest. While we are not trying to develop low success "stories," we do need to understand why the low successes were in that category, and specifically what factors impeded impact.

Table 7-1 provides a listing of the methods that we have commonly used to sort surveys into success categories, and provides an explanation for each survey of how that method addresses a particular study purpose.

Table 7-1 Methods for Using Survey Scores to Sort Respondents into Success Categories

Sorting Approach	When to Use It
1. Identify a few of the very top-most scores as the successes.	You simply need to capture and document a few of the most dramatic Success Cases that illustrate the "best" that the program is achieving.
2. Identify the very top and very bottom scores as the successes and non-successes, respectively.	You want to illustrate the impact of the program, and also to explore factors that seem to support and inhibit success.
3. Sort the respondents into demographic or other categories (job role, organizational unit, types of impact). Then identify the highest (and possibly lowest) scores in each category.	You want to illustrate and/or analyze impact in each of several different organizational units or other categories (for example, employees who are very new versus long-tenured employees).
4. Sort scores into categories that define varying levels of success or applications that led to different sorts of impact that vary according to their value to the organization.	You not only need to illustrate impact, but also to report the numbers or proportion of participants who used the learning to achieve impact.

Choosing Interviewee Candidates

In approaches 1, 2, and 3 above, the sorting process results directly in the selection of the specific interview candidates, since you are identifying the top-most and bottom-most respondents, and thus you will interview all of these.

Approach 4 from Table 7-1 is the most common SCM approach we use, and this leads to a different interview candidate-selection process. In this approach, we are trying to make reliable estimates of the proportion of success, or lack of it, that the training has achieved. We want, for example, to draw conclusions such as "32% of the trainees used their learning in ways that led to an increase in sales," or "26% of the trainees did not use their learning in any ways that led to positive results." In this case, depending on the numbers of people in the entire training population and the number of respondents in the "high-success" category, we may be dealing with relatively large pools of possible success interview candidates, perhaps even several hundred in a large study. In these instances, to be able to make reliable estimates of the proportion of true and valuable impact among this candidate pool, we have to draw a random sample for interviews. A random sample allows defensible extrapolations and estimates to be made about the larger population of success candidates.

As an example, imagine that we had conducted a study of 200 trainees who completed a management development program. Assume further that we had a total of 50 survey respondents that were above the "high-success" cut-off score, and thus our pool of possible high successes is 50 persons. We now have to decide how many candidates from this total pool to include in our sample for interviews. To some extent, this number will be driven by our budget; how much money and time we have to spend on this high-success interview proportion of the SCM study. And importantly, this number should be driven by good sampling practices. That is, we need a large enough random sample that we can make reasonable and defensible extrapolations to the larger population of all 50 respondents in this high-success category. A sample of approximately 30% should be large enough to meet our needs, and thus we might draw a random sample of 15 respondents from the group of 50 respondents, and this would be our interview sample. If this group of trainees were relatively homogenous (all sales reps, for example), then we could use a smaller sample yet of perhaps ten, or a 20% sample, and still be on safe extrapolation grounds.

One question that we are often asked by new practitioners is, "What do you do if approach 4 yields really small populations of high-success candidates?" Consider, for example, a study in which we evaluated the impact of a distance-learning sales program on automobile dealership sales staff. When we looked at the survey results, only one (1) of 100 survey respondents fell into the high-success category; 60 were in the low-success category, and the remaining 39 or so were in between.

We first had to identify the possible sources of these skewed results. One possibility was that the program was really not creating value and our cut-off criteria were correct. The other major possibility was that the program was creating more value than the survey data showed, but our cut-off scores were wrong. To determine the "truth" of the situation, we took three steps:

1. We interviewed the sole high-success candidate.

2. We drew a random sample of ten non-successes and interviewed them all to determine if they were really low-success participants. (We selected a larger sample than normal, since so many of our participants fell into this category.)

3. We selected a random sample of eight (8) "in-betweens" and interviewed them. We did this to determine if potentially incorrect cut-off scores were concealing true, or otherwise worthy, high-Success Cases.

What we found through the interview process was that the program really was not working well at all and our cut-off scores were accurate. The program was intended for sales managers, but most of the partici-pants were dealership salespeople—the course's purpose was generally misunderstood and the wrong audience was participating. There was no opportunity for application of learning and business impact.

In another study with similar results (hardly any reported "successes") we found that our cut-off scores for the high successes had been too tough; our interviews of cases selected from a group of cases we had initially scored as "low or probably non-successes" turned out to have produced relatively worthwhile results from their training.

Analyzing Data to Estimate Nature and Scope of Impact

The second key purpose of survey data analysis is to look across all survey respondents and summarize the distribution of scores so that you can make useful estimates of the scope of impact; for example, stating that "26% of all trainees used their learning to achieve positive results."

- Only two types of analyses are needed in the vast majority of cases: frequency distributions and cross-tabulations. The first of these, frequency distributions, analyze the frequency (expressed as a percentage and/or a count) with which participants selected a specific answer to a survey item.

For example, an item asking, "After training, to what extent did you establish a development plan?" might have a distribution of responses such as:

- Already had a plan (5%),
- Did not have a plan and have not established one (15%),
- Established a plan and do not expect to see results (10%),
- Established a plan, but it's too early to see results (15%), and
- Established a plan and have seen one or more positive results (55%).

Frequency distributions provide important data across all respondents of what the most frequent experience has been on an issue. These data in turn are the basis for study findings. For example, we might develop a finding that says, "About one third of trainees (36%) reported developing business plans as a result of training that in turn led to a positive business outcome such as increased revenues or reduced costs." Note, however, that we would only report this finding if we had verified the survey data with interviews and determined both the false-positive rate and the typical nature of outcomes achieved. That is, the survey results may have shown that 60% of respondents claimed a positive outcome, but the interview analysis may have shown that of these, only a few more than half turned out to be legitimate and documentable Success Cases.

The second type of descriptive statistic used in SCM survey analysis is the cross-tabulation. A cross-tabulation expresses the frequency distribution of one item from the survey for a subgroup of respondents as defined by a second item on the survey. We can show, for example, the responses to a question about the extent of development planning for each of several job role categories. The data in a cross-tabulation is often displayed in a table, such as in Table 7-2, below.

Table 7-2 Sample Frequency Distribution: Plan Development by Role

	Already had a plan	Did not develop a plan	Developed a plan; do not expect results	Developed a plan; too early for results	Developed a plan; saw positive results
Executive	2%	1%	0%	1%	1%
Manager	2%	2%	1%	5%	5%
Individual Contributor	1%	12%	9%	9%	49%

These two types of descriptive statistics are all the statistical analyses needed for the vast majority of SCM studies. Occasionally a highly complex study might require some use of inferential statistics, but these are extremely few and far between; with the low cost of e-mail and Web-based surveys, we almost never use sampling methods to access portions of trainee populations.

Chapter Eight

Digging Out and Telling the Stories—the SCM Interviews

*T*his chapter deals with the heart of the SCM: finding out what stories there are to be told about training impact, and documenting them in a valid and credible way. Because you will tell only a few stories, you want to be sure that these few are the absolute best stories. You need to document these stories objectively and completely so that they will not lose their persuasive power because they are not credible or cannot be defended as accurate and truthful.

The steps in completing your Success Case stories are as follows:

1. Plan the interview process and the questions you will ask.

2. Conduct your interviews.

3. Document the most interesting and noteworthy stories.

The following pages of this chapter expand on and illustrate each of these steps. Prior to discussing these steps in detail, we first turn to the issue of making a claim that training was the "cause" of the impact reported. A training success story is not a success story if it is likely that the behaviors and resultant outcomes that followed a training intervention cannot be causally linked to the training itself. Thus, a discussion of this issue must precede our further explanation of the interview steps themselves.

Resolving Causal Questions

The notion of causation and causal claims for events is especially problematic. It is quite simple, for instance, to make the claim that flipping on a light switch causes the light to go on. But on more consideration, one can see that there are other causes behind this apparently proximate act of flipping the switch. The cause of the light going on could be viewed as the electrical impedance that takes place in the tungsten filament inside the bulb (or the excitement of a gas in the case of a fluorescent lamp). Likewise the cause of the light going on could be attributed to the electrical generation activity that occurs at the power plant, thus enabling a flow of electrons through the wires that feed the switch. In some respects, the cause of the light going on could be the invention of the light bulb itself by Mr. Edison, as surely without this work there would be no light or electrical power plant.

To examine the considerations we must make if we are going to make a claim that training was "successful," we inevitably have to make some sort of legitimate causal argument and claim. But what will suffice? What exactly do we need to show or prove?

When we are dealing with training and the subsequent behaviors that may or may not ensue after the training, we are dealing with a complex nexus of multiple causal factors. With the SCM, we acknowledge some important assumptions:

- Any value that training may lead to is always a result of post-learning performance. Performance is always driven by a number of factors in addition to the capability to perform that training may have created; any one of these factors, such as a negative incentive or a directive to not perform, may totally overwhelm performance even when capability and a desire to perform are present.

- The results of performance (an increase in sales, an increase in employee retention, a decrease in costs, for instance) are also influenced by many external factors such as organizational changes, market conditions, and so forth.

We are left with the assumption that the only legitimate causal claim is that training was a vital catalyst in producing the behavior that in turn was a significant contributing factor to a valuable outcome.
For purposes of exploring the causal inquiry process in more help-ful detail, consider the example of a manager who received training in performance management skills and claimed in a survey to have used the training to conduct a performance review that led to concrete and worthwhile results.

Assume that some facts are already established:

- The manager participated in training in which the purpose was to equip the manager with knowledge and skills for conducting a performance review, using some new guidelines that the organization has promulgated.

- The performance review meeting was held and there was a positive outcome that ensued from the meeting: the employee and manager agreed on a performance improvement plan.

- The employee is currently engaged and making positive progress in carrying out this improvement plan.

We would like to claim that this meeting and the positive outcomes that ensued are an instance of a "success" from the training. That is, we want to claim that the training was a principal causal contributor to the positive performance review meeting and outcomes.

A Causal Analysis Framework

Our Success Case hypothesis is that the training was successful. To make this claim defensibly, we will have to eliminate some rival hypotheses. If someone could show, for example, that the manager already knew how to conduct such a review prior to participating in the training, then our success hypothesis is not supported.

Table 8-1 presents a framework, using the impact model format described in Chapter Five, that illustrates the essential logic of the training and also the several rival hypotheses that would have to be considered and then rejected if we were to claim a success from training.

Notice that the table reveals the essential logic of the training, as follows:

The participant engaged in some training and learned a new capability (skill or knowledge), the participant applied the capability acquired from the training initiative in job performance, the new or improved job performance led to or produced some results that were of value to the organization

Table 8-1 also lists below each logical element the critical questions that are "rivals" to the training success claim. Consider, for example, that we want to support a claim that a person learned, then used a new skill and that the usage led to positive outcomes that were of value to the organization. For this to be a legitimate training success instance, we would have to have present good evidence that the skill they used was indeed learned in the training and that without the training they would not have been able to use it.

We would also need evidence that the training was necessary. If for instance the person could have learned and subsequently used the skill with a simple job aid but instead they were required to attend three days of training, then we would have to qualify the "success" of this training by noting that it was unnecessarily time-consuming and complex.

Table 8-1 A Framework for Posing Alternative or "Rival" Causal Hypotheses

Impact Map Category	Key Capability	Critical Application	Performance Result	Organization Goal
Explanation	Some key SKA (skill, knowledge, or attitude) that is important for effective job performance?	An application of the skill or knowledge in some important part of the job?	An immediate outcome or result of the improved job performance?	A worthwhile goal to which the improved result makes an important contribution?
Questions to be Resolved	Was the SKA really gained from the training and not somewhere else?

Was the training necessary to acquiring the SKA; could it have been acquired in a different, cheaper and quicker way? | Was the SKA the reason for the job performance improvement?

Could the performance improvement have happened without the SKA?

Could something else (for example, an incentive, a job-aid) have just as easily produced the improved performance? | Is the improved performance really worthwhile?

Was the improved performance necessary for the result to have been produced?

Could the result have been caused by something other than the job performance? | Did the result really make an important contribution to a goal?

Is that goal truly worthwhile?

Is there any negative impact of the result? |

(continued)

Table 8-1 A Framework for Posing Alternative or "Rival" Causal Hypotheses (Continued)

Impact Map Category	Key Capability	Critical Application	Performance Result	Organization Goal
Questions to be Resolved		Is there any negative consequence of the performance (for example, is it unfair to someone, does it hurt anyone)?		

Using the Causal Analysis Framework

We use the causal analysis framework in Table 8-1 during the interview phase of a SCM study to guide questions we ask during interviews. For example, to respond to and eliminate the rival hypothesis that someone may have already had the skill that the training aimed to provide, or that someone may have learned the skill from some other source, we would ask questions such as:

"Was this a new skill for you or did you already know how to do this?"

"Where did you learn this skill that you used?"

"It sounds like this skill was helpful to you. Tell me about where you acquired it?"

Remember that our criterion for success in the SCM is that our findings would "stand up in court." We carry this judicial analogy into the interview process by adopting the conceit that we are really in a judicial setting, and that we must therefore be bound by defensible legal procedures. Accordingly, if I were to ask during this interview a question such as "This training was quite helpful, wasn't it?" then we would imagine an opposing attorney immediately jumping up and shouting "Objection! Leading the witness!" At this point, the judge would pronounce the objection sustained, and direct me to rephrase my question so that I was not presuming that the training was the source of the skill acquisition.

In this manner, we ask questions during the interview as guided by the causal analysis framework in Table 8-1 until we have convinced ourselves that we have either thoroughly eliminated the rival hypotheses or that we have failed to eliminate them, and thus must qualify our findings accordingly, admitting to uncertainty about the veracity of the success instance we are investigating.

Probing for Possible Negative Outcomes

The framework in Table 8-1 also reminds us that the effects of training and other behavior change initiatives can range from positive, to neutral, and even to negative. To qualify as a true success, a training initiative must contribute to mostly positive outcomes and certainly has to avoid any seriously negative effects.

Consider, for example, some performance management training that was provided to new supervisors. We found that some managers were using only the behavior of providing feedback about performance to subordinates and were not using the coaching skills that were also taught. The overall consequence, because these same people were not getting any coaching to help them improve, was negative. By conducting interviews with some of the subordinates, we discovered that their performance had further deteriorated since they had developed hostile and negative reactions toward their supervisors and the organization.

In another case, all managers were required to participate in training. Because the training was mandatory for all managers regardless of their background, we were careful to include an item on the survey that had the response choice: "I already had this skill and was already using it." When a large percentage of trainees responded to this choice we probed in interviews to confirm if they indeed had and were already using the skills. We concluded that, even though the training worked well with people who needed it, it was also creating a good deal of negative reaction among attendees who felt forced to go through training that they did not need.

The SCM Interview Structure

Typically, there are two principal types of SCM interviews:

- The probable high-success interview
- The probable low- or no- success interview

The High-Success Interview

The main purpose of this interview is to capture the nature and scope of the success and to document exactly how the training was used. This interview also aims to identify the factors that supported the success, and to determine the extent to which the training was a significant causal element.

This interview follows the structural flow indicated in Table 8-2.

Table 8-2 Principal Structure of a Probable High Success Interview

Interview Element	Purpose
Opening	Introduce the interviewer and put the interviewee at ease, note the purpose for the call, assure confidentiality.
Qualification	Pinpoint the best example of a successful application of learning that was achieved by this person. (If there were several, pursue the most valuable.)
	Assure that there is indeed a success here worth pursuing, that is, determine that this is not a false-positive.
	Assure that there is at least a general causal connection, that there was some element of training that was learned and applied positively.

(continued)

Table 8-2 Principal Structure of a Probable High Success Interview (Continued)

Interview Element	Purpose
Probing and Documentation	Dig into the application and results.
	Surface and describe exactly what training was used, how it was used, and to what results it led.
	Confirm the value of the results.
Identification of Support Factors	Identify and understand the role of critical systemic factors that supported the application of the training, for example, timing of the training, role of the manager, feedback, and incentives.
	Identify how this person was selected or otherwise enrolled in the training and what, if any, preparation they did for the training.
Final Exploration and Resolution of Causal Issues	Explore deeper "rival hypothesis" assumptions; define and describe causal qualifications.
Identification of Follow-Up Needs	Determine if there is a need for documentation or follow-up with other parties for confirmation.
Closing	Arrange for follow-up call if more information needed.
	Thank the person for the time given.
	Assure the person again of the confidentiality of all information.

The Probable Low- or No-Success Interview

The major aim of this interview is to identify and describe the factors that impeded application, explaining why this person did not apply the training or why the training application failed to work. This interview follows the structural flow depicted in Table 8-3.

Table 8-3 Principal Structure of the Low- or No-Success Interview

Interview Element	Purpose
Opening	Introduce the interviewer and put the interviewee at ease; note the purpose for the call; assure confidentiality.
	Assure the interviewees that they are not a rare exception, in order to put them at ease and reduce any possible negative stigma.
Probing and Documentation	Dig into the reasons why this training was not applied, was not useful, was not effective, and so forth.
	Identify how this person was selected or otherwise enrolled in the training
Identification of Follow-Up Needs	Determine if there is a need for follow-up with other parties for confirmation.
	Arrange for follow-up call if more information is needed.
Closing	Thank the person for the time given.
	Assure the person again of the confidentiality of all information.

Non-Response Follow-Up

When overall response rates are lower than about 60%, there is a strong risk of a sampling bias. In these cases, we don't know anything about the people who did not respond, and thus we can't be sure if and to what extent a bias may be influencing the return rate. To resolve this issue, we can draw a small random sample of the people who did not respond at all to the survey. (Remember, we have the names of all survey invitees because we sent them a letter or an e-mail message inviting the participation.) The purpose of these interviews is simply to put the non-respondents into a category, determining if they were mostly a success or a non-success. If the proportions of success and non-success among non-respondents are about the same as these proportions in our sample of respondents, then we assume that no bias was at work, and that the tendency to non-response is essentially randomly distributed. But if, for example, we found that 80% of non-respondents were non-successes while only 40% of our actual responses were in that category, then we would infer that a response bias is at work and that there are more non-successes in our overall population of trainees than our returned sample is showing.

We can assess the bias with interviews of a random sample of the non-respondents or we can try to do the same task with an e-mail survey. In either case, we simply ask a few questions that will allow us to categorize the person either as a successful user or as a non-successful user of the training.

Preparing for the Interviews

Once you have decided which people you are going to interview as potential Success Cases, you need to prepare a general plan for proceeding and an interview protocol. Following are some of the usual planning elements that bear attention:

Number of interviewers: One interviewer gives the highest amount of reliability in the interview process, since multiple interviewers may conduct interviews differently, thereby biasing the data. Use the lowest amount of interviewers possible to get the most reliability and consistency among interviews, while balancing workload demands.

Telephone versus face-to-face interviews: Telephone interviews are easier to schedule, cheaper, are more convenient for interviewees, and are equally productive and accurate when compared to face-to-face interviewing. Using two interviewers at a time can be very helpful for note-taking and post-interview discussion.

Length of interviews: High success interviews typically take 35 to 50 minutes; no-success interviews usually take 10 minutes or so. We plan 90 minutes for each interview to allow time to prepare (read over the survey, and so forth), complete the call, and especially to thoroughly review and write up notes.

Note-taking: Take notes as you go, summarize often, and review and write-up notes immediately afterwards. We never tape-record, as this inhibits interviewees and doubles the time needed for completion, as you must listen to the tapes. Instead, take good notes.

Soliciting and preparing interviewees: Send a communication to the interviewees you select, preferably from a senior leader, soliciting their agreement to an interview. Note that the purpose of the interview is to discuss their training experience in more detail, and firmly stress the absolutely confidential nature of the interview. Provide a means (for example, a reply e-mail) for interviewees to indicate the best time to call them for the actual interview.

The Interview Protocol

Once you have completed your general plan, you are ready to prepare the form you will use to guide the interview process and remind you of the questions you will ask. The complexity, structure, and detail of the interview protocol will depend on several factors:

- The skill and experience level of the interviewers: In general, the more expert and experienced your interviewers are, then the less detailed and structured a protocol you will need. However, we have found that it is usually best to use as little structure as possible, encouraging interviewers to conduct a natural conversation whose flow is dictated by the conversational style and direction of the interviewee.

- The number of interviewers to be involved: If only one, or a very few, interviewers are to be used in the study, it is less likely that a highly structured protocol will be needed. On the other hand, a high number of interviewers raises the likelihood of unreliability and inconsistency among the interviewers, in which case a highly structured protocol is called for.

- The complexity or uniqueness of the intervention or program that is being studied: Some Success Case studies are conducted to assess the impact of very relatively simple innovations, programs or interventions with which we, the study directors, are already very familiar. On the other hand, the program we are studying may be very complex, with many permutations and variables, or may be unfamiliar (or both!). In these sorts of instances, a more structured protocol will be needed, to remind the interviewer of questions to ask, and to include references to the many parts and nuances of the program being studied.

Filling Buckets: The Protocol Conceptual Model

It is very useful to imagine the interview process as a "bucket filling" process. In this imaginary conceit, the interview process aims to fill several information buckets, each bucket representing a certain category of Success Case information. Figure 8-1 portrays the entire Success Case interview framework as four information buckets. Overall, the interviewer needs to ask questions and guide the conversation to "fill" each bucket with sufficient information about that category. When each bucket is sufficiently filled, the interview is complete.

Figure 8-1 Four Success Case Interview Buckets

Each information bucket is a general information category. Within each of the four categories ("buckets"), more specific information is as follows:

Bucket 1: This category includes the "what, when, how, and where" questions. How did they apply the training being studied in the SCM inquiry? With whom did they use it? When? Under what conditions or circumstances was it used? What parts of the training were used the most, the least, or not at all? What evidence is there that they really did what they say they did?

Bucket 2: What valuable outcome(s) did their use of the training help achieve? Why are these results important? What business goals were contributed to? What measurable difference was achieved? How do they know they made a difference (for example, who noticed, what feedback did they get, what changed)? What evidence is there that they really achieved what they say they did? What value (dollar or otherwise) are the results worth?

Bucket 3: What in their personal repertoire or environment did they use or access that helped them? Were there any special incentives, rewards, job objectives, work requirements, and so forth, that contributed to their success? What about their manager's support (or lack of it) helped or hindered? What tools, references, information sources, or job aids did they use? How did they get into the training, and why? What seemed to differentiate them from others who did not make such successful use? What priorities, urgencies, or other extenuating circumstances spurred them to success?

Bucket 4 (optional): What suggestions (additional program resources, better tools, better incentives, more training, etc.) does the interviewee have to increase success? What suggestions can the interviewer make for improvement? (These may be based on intuition, hunches, cross-interview observations, and so forth.)

The principal advantage of this simple interview protocol is its flexibility. Using the bucket structure, we can allow the interviewees to start where they are most comfortable, allowing the conversation to be more natural and spontaneous. An interviewee might, for instance, begin to talk about a barrier, saying, for example, "I had a hard time getting started with that new laptop because my software package wouldn't work with my machine." The interviewer would simply begin making notes on the "Barriers" bucket page, then gently steer the conversation from there to other information categories.

The Non-Success Protocol

Using the same bucket structure, we can also create a protocol for the instance where we are interviewing people who were especially non-successful. In these cases, the interview structure is even simpler. Figure 8-2 shows the bucket structure for this special non-success interview.

Figure 8-2 Non-success interview buckets

Notice that this non-success protocol has only two buckets. Because this interview is conducted with persons whose survey results reported virtually no usage at all of the innovation under study, the buckets asking about what was used and what success resulted are not included. In this more focused and brief interview your principal challenge is to find out what went wrong; what got in the way of using the training, and why it was not productively used or used at all.

Conducting the non-success interview requires some special sensitivity, in that the person being interviewed should not be made to feel defensive. We usually start this interview with a sentence or two to this effect: "Our survey showed that several people were not able, for one reason or another, to do anything much with this training program. As a person who didn't get much value from this effort, what can you tell me about what went wrong? Why didn't this seem to work for you?" As the graphic in 8-2 shows, the non-success interview seeks simply to learn about what factors impeded success, and (optionally) what suggestions can be made that would have helped create a more successful experience. It is also important to determine the extent to which a failure of learning might have impeded success. Maybe the person did not use the training because he or she did not master the skills in the first place.

Documenting Success Cases

The interview process ends with formalizing and documenting the Success Cases you decide to include in your final report. This may be all of the true Success Cases you find, or it may be only a selected few that best illustrate and "tell the story" of the innovation you are studying. Probably the best way to discuss Success Case documentation is to provide an example of a Success Case "story."

Figure 8-3 contains an example of an actual Success Case impact profile (our name for a Success Case story). The setting in this instance is a field office for an international development and adoption agency in rural Zimbabwe, Africa. As you will see, this impact profile uses names of people (fictionalized) to add dramatic value. The impact profile also refers to actual dollar figures to illustrate the business value of the management development program. In this case, the agency had spent considerable resources in providing training and technical assistance to indigenous field-office managers. One of the program goals was to promote native persons into positions of leadership and provide them resources to be successful. At the same time, however, a "hard line" faction of the agency's international governing board had insisted that the support program had to "pay its own way." They wanted to see hard evidence that demonstrated the economic value, if any, of the program.

Impact Scenario #1—Eva Ibay, Operations Manager, Highland Village (Zimbabwe) Field Office

Eva attended "Leading at ABC" in the capital city in November 1997 with three professional staff in the operations department of her Field Office.
The impact findings are:
Impact at a Glance . . .

- Backlog reduced
- New enrollments were increased
- Office procedures were improved
- Return on training investment to date:
- For entire office: $82,700
- Per trainee: $20,675

(continued)

The Impact Story

During the workshop Eva and her staff talked over dinner about their plans for applying the "Leading at ABC" training. They agreed that reducing communication backlogs was their biggest problem. They were receiving low audit scores each quarter, and constant communication pressure was taking time away from working on new enrollment work. Three weeks after returning from "Leading at ABC" training, Eva had a group meeting with her professional staff and they discussed the issues they faced in reducing backlogs. They realized that the three support staff members they worked with could probably play a larger role in organizing communications, and decided to meet with them to engage them in some joint problem solving. At this session, the support staff agreed that there was more they could do, and were anxious to play a larger role.

What They Used . . .

First, Eva and the professionals used the "Diagnosing Development Level" process in a group meeting with the support staff and reached agreement on styles and situation. At their "Partnering Performance Meeting," she and the three professional staff members agreed on specific performance objectives for operations tasks and results, and on the leadership styles most appropriate for Eva.
Eva next engaged in a "Diagnosis Development" session with the three professionals. Action plans were laid out after this session, and they agreed to monitor results monthly for the next quarter.

What They Achieved . . .

After three weeks, the support staff had designed a new communications planning and monitoring system using the Lotus

(continued)

Notes software the office had recently acquired. They also designed and implemented a template for sponsor letters that greatly reduced letter preparation time. (Previously, all letters were hand-drafted individually, then typed.) Using the new system, support staff drafted letters that were then reviewed by professionals, who made revisions, and then signed off for final production.

Impact . . .

Sponsor communications backlog has been reduced 36%, and for the first time in six years, the recent audit showed the last quarter communications were fully up to date. (The backlog report showed that 30 sponsors were removed from the report.)

Eva and her staff have been able to spend an average of eight more hours per week on new enrollment initiatives.

New enrollments are 12% ahead of projections this last quarter; 26 new enrollments were completed for the period ending March 1, equaling last year's semi-annual production.

Value . . .

According to headquarter estimates, an individual sponsor delay of one quarter reduces re-sponsorship by 22%. Costs of obtaining a new sponsor are $2,600 versus $250 for retaining a sponsor, a difference of $2,350. Using this data, the value of the Highland office's backlog reduction is $70,500 (30 x $2350).

Data on the value of new enrollees is not available from headquarters but is estimated at $2,600, assuming that an applicant sponsor who is denied sponsorship because of lack of enrollees must be replaced by another applicant sponsor. Field Office records show staff time per enrollee is 3.5 hours. Using this estimate, and a total of 32 more hours

(continued)

invested per week by Eva and her three professional staff, nine of the new enrollees can be attributed to the time freed by the innovations implemented as a result of the training. The value of this improvement is $23,400 (9 x $2,600).

- Total estimated value of impact: $93,900
- Costs for training Eva and staff (includes travel, lodging, salary, pro-rata training delivery and materials costs, and so forth): $11,200
- Return on training: $82,700
- Per person (4) return: $20,675

What Helped. And What Did Not ...

Contributors:

- New computers and access to software provided by Country Office
- New audit report format instituted by Regional Director
- Permission for four staff to attend training

Barriers:

- Several planned meetings were rescheduled without notification or input from professional staff by "emergency" reports required by the Country Office.
- Support staff did not receive any incentive or reward for taking on new responsibilities; local incentives, are forbidden by ABC rules.

Figure 8-3 Example of Impact Profile with Economic Value of Impact Documented

Review Figure 8-3 and notice that the bulk of the impact profile is the impact story which is a summary narration of the Success Case. This story is just that—a brief story that describes the setting, circumstances, and the "action" (what the Success Case participant did to use the innovation, and the outcomes achieved). The story is factual, and includes references to actual facts and data.

Notice also that the impact profile follows a standard format, as follows:

- Title and identifying information
- "Impact at a Glance" (a brief summary of the overall impact)
- Immediate outcomes (the documented basic results or outcomes of the usage of the innovation)
- Business impact (the business goals and/or business value of the immediate outcomes)
- The impact story
- Background and setting
- Immediate outcomes
- Organizational impact
- What helped and what did not

Some SCM users have used audio recordings, video stories, and so forth. Readers are encouraged to innovate and try out their own formats and styles for the telling of Success Case stories. Whatever formats are used, however, should adhere to and enable the application of SCM study principles of straightforward story telling, factual references, and a plain narrative line and style.

Notice that we took pains to use estimates and calculations that were in common use within the agency. In this particular agency, adoption rates (the contribution of money by sponsors to support a needy child) were known to be linked to the backlog of outbound communications. When field offices were late or negligent in being sure that "adopted" children sent letters to their sponsors, their sponsorship rate was dramatically and negatively impacted. Armed with this knowledge, we scoured our survey results to find cases where backlog reductions had been reported, then made sure that these reductions were real, and attributable to the management development program during the interview phase.

Chapter Nine

Drawing Compelling Conclusions

T he original purpose of the SCM study drives the kinds of conclusions that should be drawn from it. This original purpose, of course, will vary from study to study. There are, however, a common range of types of conclusions that can be and are typically drawn from a SCM study. These range from the relatively simple issue of determining whether any participants in a training effort have been able to apply their learning on the job to the more complex questions of the full scope of impact, as well as value and return-on-expenses.

The Eight Major SCM Conclusions

There are eight (8) of these major types of SC conclusions, each of which is closely aligned with the SC study purposes presented earlier in the book. These types of conclusions are listed and explained briefly below, ranging from the simplest to the more complex. Then, in the pages that follow, each conclusion type is more fully described and illustrated.

The eight major types of Success Case study analysis conclusions are:

1. What if any impact was achieved? What worthwhile on-the-job applications or learning, if any, have been made by training participants? This simplest of SC purposes allows the quick gathering of evidence about the most poignant and compelling results that a training initiative is producing and provides rich illustrations of these "best-case" outcomes.

2. How widespread is success? This sort of SC study provides estimates about what numbers and proportions of program participants are using their learning. For example, this study might conclude that "60% of the participants used the program to accomplish worthwhile results that are either helping to drive more new sales, retain customers, or increase revenues-per-customer."

3. Did the training work better in some parts of the organization or with some kinds of participants than in other parts or with other people? Here we explore whether participants' roles and backgrounds appear to be a factor in explaining success, or what parts of the organization realized the greatest value from the training.

4. Were some parts of the training more successfully applied than others? Typically, we find that some methods or tools taught in the training were used more, or less, than others.

5. What systemic factors were associated with success and a lack of success? To address this question we seek information that might explain why the training was more successful in one part of the organization than another, and especially what manageable factors were most, and least, associated with success.

6. What is the value of the outcomes produced? In many cases, it is desirable and possible to attach some dollar values to learning

applications, showing, for example, that training helped drive specific increases in revenues or decreases in costs.

7. What is the unrealized impact potential of the training? Because training almost never helps 100% of the participants to be successful, we can draw conclusions about the opportunity costs associated with non-application of the training and determine what it would have been worth to the organization if more people had used their training as successfully as the most successful participants. This final type of conclusion is extremely valuable in that it enables a business case to be made for investing further resources or effort into getting more success from future iterations of a training initiative.

8. How do the benefits of training compare with costs? This type of conclusion compares the value of training outcomes to the costs, and may enable estimates of cost-benefit ratios or return-on-investment (ROI).

Rarely does an SCM study have a purpose that is so narrowly defined as to include only one or even only a few of these types of conclusions. Our SCM efforts typically include several of these types of conclusions, and thus we not only include each type of conclusion, but we point out and discuss the interrelationships among them. We often, for example include a conclusion about the value of the impact, then extend this conclusion to discuss the parts of the training that contributed most to the value, and then build on these conclusions to discuss the range of impact achieved, and from this draw conclusions about the value that could have been achieved had more participants achieved similar valuable outcomes. Finally, we would include one or more conclusions regarding the factors that contributed to achievement of results so that we could make recommendations about what the client could do to realize more value from the training. But despite the fact that these types of conclusions get combined in any one SCM study, it is still useful to explain and discuss them separately, as each conclusion requires a different sort of analysis.

Conclusion Type One: What, If Any, Impact Was Achieved?

This type of conclusion is the foundation for virtually all other SCM study conclusions. An SCM study can be viewed as a search among all of the participants in a training initiative and all of the ways that these participants might have used their training to identify the very best and most impactive applications. If this search ends up finding no worthwhile applications of learning at all, then the SCM study is pretty much over. That is, if the evidence is that no one—not a single trainee—used his or her training in a way that helped produce some valuable outcome then we need look no further for the range of impact because we already know that it is zero, and we certainly would not need to discuss the value of impacts, and so forth. In a SCM study that found no evidence of impact at all, however, we would certainly aim to draw conclusions about why there was a lack of success, searching for the factors that would explain this thoroughly miserable training outcome.

We have never, however, in several hundred evaluation studies, found a case where no one used training in at least some partially valuable way. We have certainly found a range of impact, from very little to quite a lot. In one study, fewer than 20 out of 300 people used their training as intended; in another study, more than 80% of several hundred trainees used their learning to achieve worthwhile results.

Below are some examples of this sort of conclusion as excerpted from SCM studies we have conducted:

- "The performance management training helped produce valuable results, including more clear performance objectives set in dialogues between managers and direct reports, solutions to performance problems, and increased attainment of performance objectives."

- "The training led to two types of valuable outcomes: decreased costs due to decreases in scrap rates, and increased production on key manufacturing lines."

- "Several trainees used their learning to more quickly and completely negotiate contracts."
- "Some trainees used their new marketing skills to produce marketing plans that significantly reduced the costs of external agency contracts."

Conclusion Type Two: How Widespread Is Success?

The basis for this sort of analysis is the survey data in conjunction with the interview data. In studies where samples of participants were surveyed, rather than all possible participants being surveyed, inferential statistics are applied to the survey results to make estimates of impact.

To illustrate this sort of approach to drawing conclusions, we will refer to the example of training for pharmaceutical sales reps in how to use their newly provided laptop computers. Readers should review this example in detail, as we will use it several more times, with increasing embellishments, to illustrate analysis and conclusions for other SCM study purposes.

Imagine for purposes of this example that a total of 240 representatives were provided training in how to use their new laptop computers. Consider now that the study was based on and collected the following data:

- Our survey was sent to all 240 of these sales reps, and we had usable survey responses from 200 reps.
- Of these 200 respondents, 100, or 50% reported results in the highest impact category, and were thus identified as possible Success Cases.
- 50 respondents, or 25%, reported very little or no usage of their laptops at all and were thus in the lowest category.

- The remaining 50 participants (25%) either reported some minor
  success or other partial use of their laptops, but had not yet used them in
  the most high-leverage sales applications.

To proceed with our interviews, we drew a random sample of 20
participants from the 100 people comprising the highest-scoring category. Of these 20 people interviewed, 15 of them (75% of the total of 20)
turned out to be "true positives," that is, of the 20, 15 were actually verified to have achieved results of significant value to the company through
use of their laptops. With the remaining five, we were unable to confirm
that these people were truly successful, and thus could not count them as
actual Success Cases, thus concluding that they were "false positives."

Given this information, here are the conclusions we were able to
draw about the scope of the impact of the program. Because the sample
of possible Success Cases was randomly drawn, we are able to safely assume that, had we interviewed a different sample of 20 participants, then
we would have found essentially the same results. That is, there is no
reason to believe that the 20 we actually interviewed were substantially
different from any other sales reps in the entire 100 reps in the probable
high-success population.

Conclusion #1

The laptop program has helped a total of 90 participants to be successful
in using their laptops and achieve results of significant value to the
business. This represents 37.5% of the 240 sales reps who were
participants in the laptop training program.

Basis for Conclusion #1   One hundred of the 200 participants
reported successful results. This was 50% of the sample. A random
sample of 20 of these 100 participants were interviewed and, of these,
15 (75%) turned out to be true successes. Thus, we can conclude that
75% of the participants who reported high success on their survey were

probably true successes. Inferring back to the original population of 240 we can reasonably conclude that there were probably 90 actual successful users achieving significant results.

We could not conclude that 50% of our total of 240 participants (120) represented true successes, as we know there was a false-positive rate of 25%. Thus, we reduce the reported Success Cases by 25% (that is, 25% of 120) and conclude that the training had an overall success rate of 37.5% producing 90 true high successes.

Conclusion #2

Of the 240 participants, 60, or 25%, did not make any productive use of their laptops after the training.

Basis for Conclusion #2

Of our reporting sample, 25% or 50 participants reported little to no use of the laptops, and no significant results. Calls to a random sample of 8 of these people found no false negatives. Thus, we conclude that 25% of all the trainees (25% of 240 equals 60) experienced no success at all.

Conclusion #3

The remaining 50 participants were not able to definitively achieve any significant business results from their laptops usage, though they had tried to use them in several different ways. Of these, probably half are eventually likely to achieve at least some worthwhile results.

Basis for Conclusion #3 25% or 50 trainees in our reporting sample reported that they used their laptops since the training but could not claim any definitive results yet. We made calls to a random sample of 10 of these participants and found that 5 of them reported enough laptop applications that they were likely to lead to at least some positive outcomes, though not at the same level of success as the "high" successes. The other half—5—of this random sample of non-definitive participants were clearly actually non-successes; based on their lack of application, it was unlikely that they would use their laptops to lead to any even partially worthwhile results.

We expand our no-success group by another 12.5% of the total trainee population (since half of the non-definitive respondents were actually non-successes).

So, what do we do with the 12.5% of trainees reporting only partial success? We do not add them to our high-success group, as their results were not significant enough to include them in this category. Instead, we define this category as partial or near successes; trainees who are beginning to use their laptops in ways that might eventually lead to worthwhile results. This is an important category, since we will further recommend that follow-up coaching or other support be provided to this group, because if they are not supported they are likely to regress and stop using their laptops altogether. We estimate the size of this partial success group to be also at 25%. We arrive at this estimate by adding the 12.5% discovered in our interviews of partial successes, and another 12.5% that is the group of false positives identified in the interviews of the reported high-success group.

Summary of Final Conclusions

Thirty-seven and a half percent of all the laptop trainees (90 in total) are estimated to have used their laptop training to produce worthwhile and strategically important results.

Another 37.5% (the original 25% plus the re-defined 12.5 % from the interviews of reported partial successes) probably made no worthwhile use of their laptop training at all.

Twenty-five percent are probably using their laptop training to some extent, but are not yet achieving worthwhile results, though it is likely they could do so if they received further support to sustain their progress.

Estimates of scope of impact are relatively easy to extrapolate from survey findings, and these can be further explained and corroborated from the interviews. The credibility and validity of these extrapolations is based on the soundness of the survey itself and the sampling and administration method. If one can attack the survey as an unreliable measure, or invalid because the items do not represent worthwhile results, then of course the extrapolations themselves come under question. Likewise, if samples of interviewees were not truly random, or if it can be shown that respondents did not answer truthfully and without bias, then the findings are again open to question. But, when the survey has been clearly and specifically based on an impact model that has been agreed upon and verified as faithfully representing the sought-for results, and the survey itself meets standards for good practice, and the interview sampling methods are sound, and the interviews are faithfully carried out, then the findings are reasonable and defensible.

Conclusion Type Three: Did the Training Work Better in Some Parts of the Organization or with Some Types of Participants Better than Others?

This is a relatively simple analysis that can be based on survey data alone, or can be enriched with interviews. Using survey response data, we can simply separate survey responses into each category of interest. In a recent SCM study in a large pharmaceutical company, for example, the client wanted to know if some new performance management training was being used more or less in each of three company divisions: research and development, corporate services, or manufacturing. To address this issue, we simply cross-tabulated the responses to the single summary impact item with each of the company divisions. This data summary is provided in Table 9-1.

Table 9-1 Cross Tabulated Responses to Overall Impact Survey Item in a Pharmaceutical Company SCM Study

Item: Which statement best represents your experience?	R&D	Corp Services	Manufacturing
I have used at least some of my training, and it has helped achieve a concrete and worthwhile result.	37%	42%	39%
I have tried to use some of the training but I have not been able to see any results yet.	32%	41%	43%
I have not yet used any of this training but may do so at some point.	7%	12%	9%
I already knew and was using what this training taught.	24%	5%	8%

As can be seen, overall impact was about the same in the manufacturing and corporate services divisions, and was also uniformly quite high among all of the divisions. This high rate of application was explained by the fact that engaging in at least an annual performance review was a requirement, and thus most managers in the company (the training audience) were applying the new training. But in the R&D division, there was a proportionately much larger group of manager trainees that reported to have already been doing what the training had included. On further inquiry during the interview process, we discovered that many work units in the R&D division had already adopted a similar but separate performance management process and had likewise engaged in their own separate training program related to it. Thus, we see significantly less impact from the training with this group, though it was also clear (again, from the interviews) that most of these managers were already doing a good job of performance review and appraisal. But they were not using the program being taught in the training program that was being evaluated.

Notice that, in this example, we had to combine both the survey and interview data. The survey told us one thing: there is a difference in reported application of the training. The interviews helped us verify that this apparent difference was a real difference and not just some error or bias in the data collection process. The interviews also helped us understand why the differences in impact existed—that one division had already adopted a different performance management approach. In reviewing and discussing this finding with the client, we came to understand further that such differences were common, and that there were several rather renegade subcultures among many of the R&D work units.

Conclusion Type Four: Were Some Parts of the Training More Successfully Applied than Others?

Again, this is a relatively simple sort of conclusion to draw from a SCM study. This sort of conclusion is again derived from a combination of both survey and interview data.

Consider, for example, the performance management training referred to in the previous discussion. The performance management training could have been used in several ways by managers, some more strategic and impactive than others. The client wished to know not only what outcomes application of learning might have led to, but wanted to know the different ways that the training might have been used.

Table 9-2 shows an excerpt from the survey used in this study, and also shows the distribution of responses among the several training audiences.

Table 9-2 Excerpted Data from Performance Management Training Survey

Possible Application of Performance Management Training	I tried this and achieved a concrete and positive result	I tried this but can't report any result	I have not tried this yet
Used the performance review process to conduct an annual performance review	53%	32%	15%
Used the performance review process to complete and file a performance review document	56%	34%	10%
Used the performance review process to help an employee improve performance	12%	33%	55%
Used the performance review process to help resolve a performance problem	09%	21%	70%
Used the performance review process to help an employee better understand performance objectives	45%	15%	40%

Notice that the items in Table 9-2 define and ask respondents to report on the different ways that they might have put their learning to use. There was widespread application of the learning, but only in certain narrow applications, such as conducting a required performance review and filing a performance review document. In the more strategic and impactive applications, there was far less usage.

During the interview phase of the study, we were able to uncover some very valuable outcomes that the training helped achieve for some of these more impactive applications. The client was then able to use the data quite constructively in two important ways. First, the generally widespread application of the learning was the "good news" that at least the training was getting used, if not in the most strategic ways. This at least meant that people had learned the content and were beginning to try it out. The powerful stories of the highly worthwhile results that could be achieved when the training was strategically applied (such as to improve lagging performance) were inspiring and showed the great value the training was capable of generating. This helped make a case that the training was worthwhile and could lead to positive outcomes. Further, the stories of strategic success were useful in helping latter trainees understand and become motivated to try the training in more impactive applications.

Conclusion Type Five: What Systemic Factors Were Associated with Success and a Lack of Success?

As we have seen throughout this book, being able to analyze, understand, and explain how training impact is driven by interaction with systemic factors is a principal purpose and benefit of the SCM approach. Thus, it is likely that this type of conclusion will be pursued in all SCM studies.

The data for this type of conclusion are derived from the SCM interviews. The interviews of non-successes, of course, are aimed solely at trying to understand why training was not applied. We focus intently on trying to understand what factors kept these people from trying out their learning or not having success when they did try it. These findings will then be reported as accurately and directly as we can. Below are some examples of the conclusions we might report:

- In 70% of the instances where trainees did not apply their new training, their immediate supervisor had not been a participant in the training himself or herself.

- Half of the people (49.7%) who did not apply their training felt that the training had been provided to them too early and that by the time they had a need to make a new hire, they could not recall the human resources process steps that they should follow and that they learned in the training session.

- Fully 78% of the trainees who reported, "This training was a waste of my time," reported that their manager had not met with them to have a pre-training dialogue

- 45.8% of the managers who did not use the second half of the development planning process (having a development plan review meeting) worked in the refinery production division. On further inquiry, we discovered that the senior executives in this division had made several statements during an all-employee meeting that development planning was being postponed due to a reduction in the corporate training allocation.

When searching for systemic factors that interact with or otherwise influence training impact, we use a systems factors framework, shown in Figure 9-1. This framework is similar to those developed by performance systems and human performance technology experts such as Mager and Pipe (1997), Rummler and Brache (1995), and Gilbert (1996). SCM practitioners would be wise to refer to these sources and perhaps develop their own analytic framework to fit both their context and their previous experience and education. We use this framework to guide our questions and to be alert for the factors other than the training that we are investigating that may have influenced the performance that we are exploring in the SCM interview. Then, we analyze all of our data again (both from interviews and from the survey) in light of this or similar frameworks to help us formulate conclusions and recommendations.

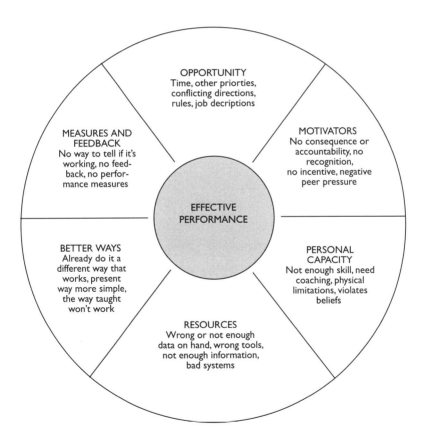

Figure 9-1 Performance Systems Factors that Interact with Training Impact

This sort of study purpose requires a bit of "detective" work to figure out the reasons for non-success. But, these sorts of conclusions are almost always quite readily available if the SCM study leader is willing to dig a little. And, they often have great value as they can salvage increased value from partially or marginally successful programs.

Conclusion Type Six: What Is the Value of Outcomes Achieved?

In several cases, we are able to estimate or otherwise calculate the monetary value of the outcomes achieved. It should be noted that we don't always do this, nor does a SCM study that does not include such estimates rank lower in importance because it does not include these estimates and calculations. But, there are instances where clients would like to have such estimates and they are likewise readily available.

In the study of financial advisors, for example, one immediate and documented outcome that was clearly attributable to the training was the increase in numbers of appointments booked by new advisors who applied some of their emotional intelligence skills. The financial services company had data on hand that allowed us to extrapolate from this outcome (increases in appointments) to create an estimate of the monetary value of the outcomes. The data showed, for example, that, on average, one sale was closed for each 12 appointments successfully booked and completed. The data also showed the dollar value of the typical first sale. A typical sale was worth $12,000 a year in fees and other revenues. A single additional appointment, then, was worth about $1,000. Or, a financial advisor who increased her appointment booking rate from an average of 12 appointments per month to 16 appointments a month, would, over a year, conduct 48 (4 additional appointments per month times 12 months); these 48 additional appointments could be projected to lead to 4 additional sales each worth $10,000. So, we could estimate that the value of the training impact in her case was about $40,000.

In SCM studies where we have randomly drawn a sample of high-success cases from the reported high successes, and also completed interviews with these people that have documented outcomes, and we have further estimated the value of those outcomes, we can make projected estimates of the value of the overall training impact. Consider the simple example below in Table 9-3 drawn from the preceding illustration of the financial advisor training.

Table 9-3 Estimate of Monetary Value of Training Program Impact

Impact Estimate	Calculation Explanation
The training program led to a success rate of 22.5 %, or 90 successful trainees.	400 people completed the training. Of these, 100 reported that they were successful. Our interviews of a random sample of these 100 documented 18 true successes, or a rate of 90%. Thus there were 90 true successes from the entire population of 400 trainees. This is 22.5 %.
The training program led to an overall impact worth $900,000 in annual revenues.	The average value of training application for each individual in the high-success group was $10,000. There were 90 people in this group, thus 90 times $10,000 equals $900,000.

For readers who may be less familiar with producing value estimates for the outcomes of training, there are several resources available. The return-on-investment (ROI) work of Jack Phillips (2003) and works by Wayne Cascio (1982) are suggested.

Conclusion Type Seven: What Is the Unrealized Value of the Training?

This conclusion involves making estimates of how much more value a program could achieve, based on the value it is currently achieving.

This purpose comes into play especially the more the following four conditions are met:

- A relatively small proportion of all participants are making successful use of training.
- Those few who are using the training are doing so with great success worth significantly more than the individual cost of engaging each one in the training.
- The SCM study has identified some of the key factors that differentiate a successful from a non-successful performer.
- At least some of these factors could be relatively easily managed to overcome their negative effect.

Unrealized value findings often lead to a readily justified proposal for a further intervention to help more participants use the innovation successfully. It is already known that the training, when used, leads to significant results. But, only a few are using it in this way, and thus there is a seemingly great upside potential for greater overall value, if only more participants could use the training. Finally, because we know what factors can be manipulated, and we have some suggestions for helping manipulate them effectively, we have the makings for a business case to justify easily a recommendation for further intervention. In this scenario, it is a relatively simple matter to estimate how many more participants we would have to help use the innovation successfully to justify the costs of our proposed intervention.

This is an extremely useful type of conclusion and should almost always be drawn even when monetary estimates of the value of the training are not calculated. If the positive applications of the training were worthwhile, even if there were no monetary estimates, then it follows that the proportion of people with whom the training did not work represent, at least to some extent, an unrealized benefit.

Assume, for the sake of a simple example, that 100 people completed a training program and that of these, 40% or 40 people used their training in ways that led to worthwhile outcomes, such as an increase in staff morale or an increase in successful performance-management meetings completed. (Notice that for this example we are intentionally avoiding a monetary estimate, as it is not germane or necessary to understand the logic of an unrealized outcome.) This obviously means that 60% did not use their training to help achieve such worthwhile outcomes.

Does this mean that the program left some unrealized value "on the table"? Perhaps yes, and perhaps no. If a training effort leads to some partial success, such as in this case with 40% achieving worthwhile results, there are two basic explanations possible, as we discussed in Chapter Two.

This training was completely and 100% effective with only these people—40% of all trainees—and the remaining 60% were somehow not capable of mastering the training outcomes or successfully using the training at all.

Some of the remaining 60% might have been able to use their training, at least partially, in equally successful ways as did the high successes had they received some further support or opportunity that the high group experienced.

As we noted in explained in Chapter Two, the latter explanation is more likely, and can also be readily confirmed from interviews with samples of high successes and near successes. These near successes from the middle of the impact distribution represent the group for whom there is probable unrealized value.

We might additionally conclude that the very bottom-most proportion of the survey response group would not have been likely to use their training under any conditions whatsoever. In some performance management training, for instance, we discovered that about 10% of the people who participated in the training had no direct reports, and thus simply could not have used the training since it taught them how to conduct performance reviews with direct reports, of which they had none. There was no performance system factor (managerial support, for instance) that we could have managed or manipulated to help them apply their learning on the job.

But it is highly likely that the remaining 50% (all of the people in the middle of the success distribution) could probably have made at least some more useful application of their training, and thus this group represents the unrealized value of the training. Some of the people, for example, got their training at the wrong time. Had they been trained at a more favorable time, then they would have used their training and achieved good results. Some other trainees received little to no support from their managers; others yet were saddled with responsibilities that prevented them from meeting with direct reports to employ the performance management tools, and so forth.

We conclude, then, that the training indeed "left unrealized value on the table." In future iterations, our client should make concerted efforts to better manage the performance factors that impeded successful results, and by doing so would gain a better return on their training investment.

We can also draw unrealized value conclusions when there are monetary estimates available. For this illustration, we return to the previous example of the emotional intelligence training for financial advisors. Recall that 22.5% of participants had used their training in ways that led to impacts valued at $900,000 overall, and an average impact per successful trainee of $10,000.

Table 9-4 displays some of the unrealized value estimates that we are able to infer from the initial estimates of the scope of findings compared with the value of impacts achieved.

Table 9-4 Unrealized Value in a Training Program for Financial Advisors.

Example Conclusion	Explanation
The training program could have achieved significantly greater value had more people used their training. The value of this additional impact that could have been achieved ranges from a very conservative estimate of $450,000 to a more aggressive estimate of $1,115,000.	Conservative estimate: If an additional 22.5% or 90 trainees were to use their training only half as well as the most successful trainees this would result in 90 times $5,000 equals $450,000. More aggressive estimate: We work to increase the overall impact rate to 80%. This projects an additional 57.5% using their training but again only half as effectively as the most successful trainees. This is 230 additional trainees achieving results worth $5,000 per trainee or a total of $1,115,000.

Notice that neither of these unrealized value estimates assumes that future iterations of the training could be made to work with 100% of the trainee population. This rather pessimistic view represents the reality that no organization is successful enough in its selection, retention, and development practices to assure that all employees could be even half as productive as the top-most 20% or so of employees. We make conservative estimates of unrealized value, and typically assume that the bottom-most proportion of the impact distribution can not be brought around through any manipulation of the performance system environment to achieve greater results. We typically assume that those more near the top of the distribution could have been helped to apply the training and become more productive, but probably not equally effectively as the top-most group, and thus we arbitrarily select an estimate of half the rate of effectiveness, projecting a more conservative figure for unrealized value.

Applying Unrealized Value Conclusions.

The concept of unrealized value is a principal benefit and leverage point for the SCM. It is always a good idea to conduct an SCM study early in the evolution of large, organization-wide training initiatives. The results can then be used to gain increasingly greater value from these future and more broad roll-outs, both by getting more results from less successful trainees and by avoiding the costs of enrolling people in the training whom the previous SCM study showed could never gain value.

Unrealized value conclusions also are helpful for selling the value of SCM studies to clients. Consider an example of a recent study in which several of the top-most successful trainees used their training to achieve results worth $60,000 each. The entire SCM study cost $30,000. If we could use the study to help just one more trainee use training only half as well as one of these most successful trainees, the evaluation was fully paid for!

Conclusion Type Eight: How Do the Benefits of the Training Compare with the Costs?

Conclusions of this type simply take the previous estimates of scope of impact and value of impact a step further, comparing these to the costs of the training itself. For the sake of simplicity and ease on the reader's imagination, the same financial advisor example will be used to illustrate this sort of conclusion.

Recall that the company put 400 financial advisors in all through the training. Of these, we were able to document 90 solid success instances worth an average of $10,000 each to the company, or a total of $900,000. We then analyzed the costs of the training, using templates and estimation procedures that are readily available for this sort of analysis (Phillips, 2001) and that take into account development and delivery costs, opportunity costs, and so forth. The result of this analysis was that the training probably cost the company about $2,000 per person on average, or a total of $800,000. Comparing the value of impact ($900,000) to this cost shows that, even with an impact rate of only 22.5%, the cost-outcome ratio was good. While the training function was happy that there had not been a net loss on the training, it was likewise clear that the training could have achieved a good deal more value for the money spent.

We intentionally avoid making true ROI estimates, since we believe the concept and language are often used inappropriately and can invite rightful suspicion and outright rejection from those audiences with strong economic training and backgrounds. Recall that it is a basic premise of the SCM that training outcomes must interact with and be supported by the right blend and set of performance system elements in order to lead to performance that in turn leads to valuable impacts. It flies in the face of this conceptual understanding, then, to partial out the costs of the training alone and calculate an ROI estimate for the "training." On the one hand, we are working hard with our clients to help them understand the complex nature of learning and performance with the longer-range goal of getting more managerial involvement in the entire process. It is not helpful, then, to turn around and make a claim for the sole and separate impact of the training, as if it alone were the key and major contributor. In our experience, training stakeholders question ROI conclusions after-the-fact and, furthermore, do not really care about them. They prefer to know whether the training is achieving worthwhile results, whether it is being conducted efficiently, and, especially, whether they are getting all of the value from it that it is capable of producing.

Together, these eight kinds of SCM conclusions form the scope of learnings that can be derived from SCM studies. As noted, a single SCM study rarely addresses all of the conclusion types, but more typically combines several of them together. The final four chapters of this book contain four actual SCM case examples, wherein readers will find many illustrations of these conclusions exemplified.

Part II

Four different case examples from recent SCM studies are presented. In the first, Conny Bauer of Copenhagen, Denmark, writes of her work with Grundfos, a major and global manufacturer and distributor of pumps and pumping systems and components. The sales training that Conny evaluated had a high rate of impact for which she was able to identify monetary estimates of value. This study was somewhat unusual in that the training had a very high rate of impact and thus there were not a lot of recommendations to be made about leveraging greater value from future efforts.

The second case is contributed by Carmie Boutin and Cheryl Brogan of Hewlett Packard, describing a very interesting SCM study that they conducted (with help from Robert Brinkerhoff and Dennis Dressler) several years ago when they were known as Compaq. This study uncovered rich and dramatic business impact, but also documented a high rate of low or no impact. Identifying the causes for the low impact added great value to this SCM study that provides at the same time an intriguing and entertaining look at the training process.

The third case study is contributed by Dennis Dressler and Scott Blanchard. This focuses on leadership training combined with individual coaching provided to the Coffee Bean and Tea Leaf Company, and again this study reported a high rate of impact. In this case, the SCM results validate the augmented learning process that was employed by the client company, showing how training can be combined with other performance-support activities to achieve very worthwhile and widespread results.

The final case is contributed by Tim Mooney of the Advantage Performance Group (APG) and Deborah Kuby of Allstate Insurance. Together, they conducted a SCM study of a business acumen program at Allstate. This case example was able to identify monetary impacts from the training and a relatively high rate of impact. But this SCM study was unusual in that it was conducted by a team of Allstate staff members led by Debbie Kuby with Tim Mooney—an SCM veteran and expert — providing guidance and assistance. Tim and Debbie discuss the issues they confronted in helping the team understand the SCM and organize their efforts to complete the study.

Chapter Ten

Sales Training at Grundfos

Conny Bauer

The Setting

With an annual production of more than 10 million pump units used for domestic as well as for industrial purposes, water-supply, and waste water management, Grundfos is one of the world's leading pump manufacturers. Grundfos Group Management is domiciled in Bjerringbro, Denmark, and has sales and production companies in all parts of the world. Annual revenues in 2003 were 1.5 billion U.S. dollars, generated by 11,700 employees.

In the late 1990s Grundfos launched a new global customer orientation strategy to become increasingly valued as a business partner to customers, not only as a supplier of pumps. The Poul Due Jensen (PDJ) Academy, a corporate training center, was established as a part of that strategy to train the sales force world wide.

Since 2001 the PDJ Academy has developed courses and trained more than 800 internal participants a year in 2 main categories: a global sales, service and marketing training program (3 modules), and product training. The PDJ Academy reflects that Grundfos believes in creating a deeper sense of belonging and understanding with each individual employee. "We do what we do because we believe that employees who understand the organization in its context are good for business," says Kim Hansen, CEO of the PDJ Academy.

In addition to measuring immediate participant satisfaction after every course the PDJ Academy measures increases in knowledge by testing the knowledge of each participant before, immediately after, and again three months after courses are completed. The PDJ Academy also conducts an annual internal customer satisfaction survey.

Still, none of the metrics used so far had been able to disclose the impact of the training to the organization, nor did any of the metrics answer the questions: How is the training transferred to the job situation? What kind of value to the business does it create? How can the training or the learning environment be adjusted in order to increase the business impact of the learning?

Purposes of the SCM Study

Kim Hansen, CEO of the PDJ Academy, tells the following story: "When the chairman of the board asked me: 'Tell me, Kim, can you promise me that the PDJ Academy will impact the bottom line?' I said 'Yes,' and felt confident doing so. Only at that time I did not know how to prove it." This was one reason why the Success Case Method (SCM) approach seemed promising and was a welcome tool at the right time.

Another reason was that Kim Hansen and his Chief Learning Officer, Henrik Jespersen, were planning visits to the international sales managers

of Grundfos companies. Some managers were reluctant to send participants to the mandatory sales course because of the time lost from sales
activities and some because they had the impression that the learning at
the PDJ Academy is very theoretical with little practical use. The purpose
of the visits was to present the business case for training: to prove the
value of the PDJ Academy to the sales organization and thereby to convince the managers around the world that taking their sales staff off their
job and sending them to Denmark for a nine day training course was a
good investment.

It seemed obvious to the CEO of the PDJ Academy, that if he could
deliver evidence that the sales training had actually helped Grundfos'
sales representatives to create economic value for their company, it would
be much easier to convince the managers that the courses were a worthwhile investment. Even better if he could give them examples of how the
training had improved the sales and how they as managers could influence the impact of the training.

Organizing the Study

Through negotiations with the CEO and CLO the decision was made to
conduct an SCM evaluation of two of the sales training programs:

- Module 1: Customer Based Communication (CBC) which is mandatory
  for all internal and external sales staff in Grundfos, and

- Module 2: Professional Business-to-Business Sales and Marketing (B2B)
  where only experienced sales staff members are eligible.

In 2003, 300 sales representatives attended the CBC program including backup, marketing, and internal sales staff, and 70 senior sales
people attended the B2B program. However, it was decided to conduct
the study only among external sales people from key markets such as

Germany, U.K., U.S.A., France, Greece, Poland, and Denmark. After this selection of the eligible population the target group was reduced to 42 CBC participants and 48 B2B participants who had completed their training in the past 12 months.

Challenges and Constraints

At that time the PDJ Academy was a bit concerned that the organization might be "fed up" with answering surveys from headquarters, and they warned us that some people might perceive surveys as a tool used by headquarters to control their behavior. As we wanted to get a high-response rate, we decided to keep the survey brief, and in the sponsor letter and the accompanying mail we decided to focus very clearly on the confidential nature of the study and on the learning purpose of the survey: That it was meant to help the PDJ Academy provide learning experiences that positively impact them and their business goals.

We were also aware of the importance of involving all stakeholders, such as local human resources functions. The PDJ Academy took over the responsibility to inform local human resources representatives about the study and the Success Case approach as a tool to invite feedback about the business impact of training and the learning environment.

As the verification of stories is a major issue, one major concern was how to verify the results reported. Of course, Grundfos collects consolidated sales figures, but the methods and levels of measuring and reporting were not immediately available without great cost and effort. We decided then to rely on the participants' own information supplemented by a survey of the participants' managers in order to verify whether the participant's perception of results was in line with his manager's.

The SCM Chronology

Preparation—Collect and Study Information

After having decided the frame and scope and the timeline for the study we collected as much information as possible and as needed about the program, the participants, and about the business and the concerns of the stakeholders.

We studied the curriculum of the CBC and the B2B programs, the instructional methods used and a list describing the "everyday situations, where participants can improve" based on the learning outcomes for the CBC course.

We also collected data about the participants, as we did not want to ask people about background information which we could extract from the company database.

We studied the participant satisfaction and customer satisfaction evaluation sheets completed for these courses in order to avoid duplicate questions and to supplement the information and measures, which were already available.

Finally we studied the structure and history of the company and some available market and industry information in order to get an understanding of the business environment in which the sales staff operates.

The Impact Model

Since a major purpose of the study was to make a business case for the training, it was vital that we understood the business context and exactly how the program might, if it were successful, lead to business value.

While we created impact models for both the CBC and the B2B program, for the sake of simplicity from this point on we will provide detailed descriptions of our SCM planning steps only for the CBC program. We created several drafts of the impact model that we then reviewed with key stakeholders to check for the accuracy of our analysis. The impact model format was easy for these stakeholders to understand, and thus the reviews were brief and productive. Our final impact model for the CBC program is shown as Table 10-1 below.

Table 10-1 Impact Model CBC

Participants	Knowledge + Skills	Critical Applications	Improved Results	Business Goals
External Sales Representatives • Wholesale • Process industry • Water supply and waste water • CBS plus DBS (Commercial or Domestic Building Services)	Understand the delivery cycle and how to use it	Better utilize the production and delivery facilities	Improved supply-chain management	Sales target met or exceeded
	Learn how to apply e-business tools	Introduce e-tools (wincap, webgold . . .) to clients	More clients who solve minor problems or questions on web	Increased client satisfaction
	Networking	Sustain regular contact with colleges in other companies	Increased performance through knowledge sharing	
	Master time planning Learn how to structure sales efforts Understand how to use important facts, measurements, loyalty indicators	Optimized effective time with customers Work goal-oriented	Increased number of new clients	

(continued)

Table 10-1 Impact Model CBC (Continued)

Participants	Knowledge + Skills	Critical Applications	Improved Results	Business Goals
External Sales Representatives • Wholesale • Process industry • Water supply and waste water • CBS plus DBS (Commercial or Domestic Building Services)	Learn sales communication techniques Extend ways to respond to resistance • Learn to tell good potential clients from less valuable clients • Learn how to sell "Grundfos" according to the Grundfos branding concept instead of just products * Understand business strategies	Better target sales points to client needs and to client values Better detect real client needs in relation to the products, services, and benefits we offer Improve customer dialog • Prioritize potential customers • Less focus on price discussions • More focus on cooperation and mutual benefits	Increased number of new clients • Reduced time wasted on "blind" leads and low-revenue clients • Reduced number of calls per meeting • Reduced number of client contacts per sale • Reduced number of orders lost because of price • Increased scope of cooperation with existing clients • Increased value of contribution from clients • Higher customer retention	Sales target met or exceeded Increased client satisfaction

Survey

We faced a challenge in creating and presenting the survey instrument so that it would not be seen by respondents as a performance control tool or in any other way viewed as management trying to "check up" on sales people's performance. We decided to use very few questions for the surveys and to construct them so that they focused only on applications of learning that our impact model showed to be most tightly linked to the desired business results.

We reviewed draft versions of the survey with key stakeholders and made appropriate revisions. Note that this survey also contained some items about the person's role and tenure with Grundfos, as well as some items about factors that may have helped or hindered their training. In this case, the client wanted to know about the factors across all training participants, thus we included this as a survey item instead of relying solely on the interview process to learn about these factors.

The CBC survey is shown below as Figure 10-1.

CBC: Participant Survey

Please complete the survey by clicking the button which best suits your answer. When finished, click the "Submit" button.

Part A: Background
1. How much total sales experience do you have?

☐ Less than a year
☐ 1–3 years
☐ 4–5 years
☐ 6–10 years
☐ Over 10 years

(continued)

2. What segment(s) are you working with?

☐ Industry
☐ Water supply and waste water
☐ Building services

3. What year did you join Grundfos?

☐ ☐ ☐ ☐

Part B: Application of Training

4. Based on the skills you acquired in the CBC training course, which of the following skills have you successfully applied? (Check all that apply.)

☐ Structure your sales efforts
☐ Engage in dialog about delivery conditions
☐ Implement personal time management
☐ Introduce Grundfos e-tools to clients
☐ Talk more "Grundfos" and less "products"
☐ Practice active listening
☐ Match clients' needs and values
☐ Handle price discussions
☐ Share knowledge with colleagues in other companies

5. Using the skills you've applied from the CBC training, what business results have you achieved? (Check all that apply.)

☐ Increase your personal sales results
☐ Overcome customer resistance
☐ Reduce time spent per sale
☐ Reduce time wasted on "blind" leads
☐ Reduce number of orders lost due to price
☐ Reduce discount sales
☐ Improve the delivery flow from factory to client

(continued)

6. Overall, how much impact did the CBC training have in helping you to produce valuable and measurable business results?

☐   No impact

☐   Little impact

☐   Not sure

☐   Moderate impact

☐   High impact

Part C: Factors That Drive Success or Non-Success

7. What factors (if any) helped you use the training experience from the CBC course effectively? (Check all that apply.)

☐   My solid understanding of the skills learned in the course

☐   My belief that the training will improve my results

☐   Discussion with my manager about how CBC would help me and help our business to be successful

☐   Availability of support from the PDJ Academy

☐   Planned time and resources to implement CBC

☐   Work environment in which learning and knowledge sharing is valued

☐   Knowledge sharing with other participants in the CBC course

☐   Favorable market opportunity

☐   Follow-up discussions and coaching with my manager

8. What factors (if any) hindered your ability to implement the training experience from the CBC course effectively? (Check all that apply.)

☐   My incomplete understanding of the skills learned in the course

☐   My feeling that the training will not improve my results (irrelevant in my current position/market focus)

☐   Lack of clear management support for the training

☐   Lack of follow up support from PDJ Academy

(continued)

> ☐ Lack of planned time and/or resources
> ☐ Work environment that discourages learning and knowledge sharing

Figure 10-1 Grundfos CBC Survey Form

Before we distributed the survey, all participants received an e-mail from the CEO of the Academy introducing the purpose of the survey, asking for their candid feedback and response and pointing out the confidential nature of the survey.

Then the survey was distributed by e-mail directly from the evaluation team with a cover note again pointing out that the survey is confidential and allowing for two weeks' time to answer.

The survey was sent to 42 CBC and 48 B2B participants. After 2 weeks we sent a reminder, so that we ended up with a response rate of 76% from CBC and 90% from the more senior B2B participants.

The responses to the key impact questions are shown in Table 10-2 below.

Table 10-2 Responses from the CBC and B2B Participants Regarding Training Impact

"Overall, how much impact did the CBC training have in helping you to produce valuable and measurable business results?"

	Count	Percent
High impact	6	19%
Moderate impact	13	40%
Not sure	5	16%
Little impact	6	19%
No impact	0	0
No answer	2	6%
Total	32	100%

(continued)

Table 10-2 Responses from the CBC and B2B Participants Regarding Training Impact (Continued)

"Overall, how much impact did the B2B training have in helping you to produce valuable and measurable business results?"

	Count	Percent
High impact	10	23%
Moderate impact	26	60%
Not sure	2	5%
Little impact	5	12%
No impact	0	0
No answer	0	0
Total	43	100%

As can be seen, most respondents reported either high or moderate impact. No respondents reported no impact at all, however nearly 20% of the CBC group and 12% of the B2B group reported achieving only little impact. These latter respondents were considered the "low" success candidates while the high and moderate reporting respondents were considered as success candidates.

Selecting Candidates

Based on this question we identified candidates for interviews, primarily seeking candidates among the "high" and "little" impact. However, we realized that we might need to talk to more people to get enough really solid impact stories. In order to get input from all three Grundfos business segments (industry, building, and water) we made arrangements to interview 11 CBC participants: 5 high impact, 2 moderate impact, and 4 little impact. We also arranged interviews with 11 B2B participants: 6 high, 2 moderate, and 3 little. If we did not get an interview with our first choice candidate, we looked for somebody with approximately the same profile.

In order to structure the interviews and make sure everybody was given a chance to reflect on the same main issues, we followed an interview protocol, still leaving plenty of room for individual examples and reflections. We referred to the interviewee's survey responses during the interview, saying, for example, "You indicated in the survey that you _____. What did you mean by that? Can you give an example?"

We also probed with each interviewee to be sure that there was indeed a defensible argument to be made that the training was the key catalyst for the behavior and impact reported, asking a question such as: "How do you know that the success is linked to the training?" then following with probing questions to be sure that there was a plausible link to the training.

The interviewees were sales people from Denmark, Germany, UK, Poland, France, Spain, Italy, Greece, and the USA. Their English ability was mixed. Given some of the English speaking difficulties with some interviewees we decided that two people should listen to each interview to make sure that we understood all the important details we asked about.

Conducting Interviews

The interviews were conducted over a period of two weeks. It turned out that we need not have been concerned about building trust. Once people grasped the purpose and method and started reflecting over the link between the skills they had used and the results they achieved all interviewees were willing to tell their stories and share their thoughts without fear or reservation. Assured of the confidentiality of the information, they provided all the information we needed in order to qualify them as genuine Success Cases: exact details about dates and places, names of customers, contacts, and companies, competitors, the amount of sales per type of pumps, growth in currency and percent, and so forth. We were right to assume that professional sales staff normally know their sales figures; however, it turned out that the timing was perfect. The interviews were conducted at the time when several participants were having annual job development interviews with their managers, so they were updated and very precise about their performance figures.

We decided—and the PDJ Academy agreed—that with such detailed and precise information about results and performance, there was no need to insist on further documentation from the individual companies, especially since we had conducted a survey among the managers of the participants which confirmed the business impact of the training. The identity of the participants or the names of customers were not disclosed to Grundfos. However, Grundfos did recognize the types of pumps referred to in the individual cases.

Results

A safe conclusion is that based on the success scenario as reported and documented by the SCM study, the sales training at the PDJ Academy does not only cover the costs of running the whole activity with 850 course participants a year, but also contributes significantly to the sales success of the operating companies.

One of the key strategic goals defined in the impact model was to "meet or exceed sales target." A very conservative calculation indicates that 10 verified cases reported by people who have attended the CBC or the B2B program have generated 30 million DKK (Denmark Kroner) worth of extra sales that can be attributed to their application of skills and methods learned in the training. This figure is very interesting because it means that the first year after training these 10 people alone had generated enough extra sales to cover the total annual costs of running all of the PDJ Academy sales development courses.

However, the value generated by the PDJ Academy is no doubt much higher. The survey showed that 18 CBC respondents (56%) and 27 B2B respondents (62%) had increased their sales using various techniques taught in the programs. As 10 participants alone pay the total cost of running the Academy, the results of the remaining 25 sales people has direct bottom line impact.

CBC Results According to the survey data, 60% of the CBC participants said the training had high or moderate impact on measurable business results. According to a survey among their managers, they were even more positive about the overall business impact of the training. 72% of their managers claim to have registered high or moderate business impact. During interviews participants described in detail how they have used a variety of the CBC-supported techniques and behaviors successfully on the job.

Six CBC participants (19%) reported "little impact." The interviews shed some light on the reason why. A service person reported that he had enjoyed the course very much and benefited from active listening, time management, and negotiation techniques in his private life. However, he had no intention of going into sales and did not know why he was "sent" to the course. He felt that since he could not report much business impact, it might not justify a nine-day residential training session. Technically, this person should have been excluded from the target group of the survey, which was limited to external sales people. However, service personnel are invited to the CBC course, and his case demonstrates the attitude (and gratitude) on one hand and the limited business benefit on the other hand. For internal staff attending the mandatory course, "success" cannot be measured by the same parameters as for external sales staff.

The interview was also used to identify the major factors that enabled success. Not surprisingly the most frequently identified were management support, planned time to practice, inspiring training methods as well as contact with other Grundfos staff, and, most of all, their own attitude to learning. Likewise the barriers mentioned were poor English skills, cultural differences in management styles, and lack of time and support to implement the learning.

Impact Profiles

In order to be eligible as a "Success Case" the interviewees must be able to tell exactly how they have used the training to create results, and exactly what kind of results they achieved. The five CBC interviews (impact profiles) included in the impact report were chosen because they were well-documented, but also because they demonstrated different kinds of success strategies used in different business segments.

One of the participants in the mandatory CBC course was so impressed by the training, the training facilities, and the attention invested in him that he claimed "high impact" in his survey. However, in the interview he was not able to give any verifiable example of how he put the training to practical use. Such a person is an excellent ambassador for Grundfos and certainly a valuable employee, but he is not considered a "Success Case" in the methodological meaning of the word.

As in other SCM applications, we had to dig deep to try to make a connection to the training and remove doubt as to the causes of success. For example, one sales person reported "high impact" since the course. It turned out that he had been contracted to supply pumps in connection with the Olympics in Greece in 2004. Although his growth in revenue was well documented and quite impressive and although he obviously was very precise with names and dates, he could not convincingly tie this "success" to the application of any special learning from the CBC course. One would expect in this case that the market conditions were the overwhelming factor for success. Therefore this case was not considered valid documentation for the business impact of CBC, and was not accepted as one of the impact profiles.

The following example summarizes one of the impact profiles included in the report. This participant tells how he used the "mapping" technique taught in the training to secure a new four to five year framework agreement for Grundfos worth 250.000£ per year: His contact with one account was a very forceful character who had given him an extremely rude welcome at their first meeting. The interviewee realized that there was a lot of money and prestige at stake if he could penetrate this account and there was no way around this person. He was the gatekeeper to other important sponsors. So after the CBC program he made a new approach using the techniques learned in the program. After several meetings he managed to secure the new framework agreement with an additional potential for selling other Grundfos products. His own judgment is that without the CBC course he would not have been able to improve that relationship. He said: "I would have lost the order to a competitor. The course reminded me, in a fresh and different surrounding, how I can use the skills—some of which are common sense—as an important sales tool. The role plays were very helpful in creating a correct analysis of this difficult account contact."

B2B results Among the more senior participants in the B2B course 83% reported high or moderate impact on their business results. We were able to work out that people with more than six years' sales experience and Grundfos seniority benefit the most from B2B. Around 62% increased the volume and the value of their sales results, and the five participants verified in their interviews that they had increased their revenues by 25 million DKK using specific B2B learning, such as negotiation techniques, value-added selling, more focus on segmentation of customers, and so forth.

B2B participants also found it valuable to meet other Grundfos professionals at the PDJ Academy, because it gave an idea of the scope of knowledge resources available worldwide. These participants were equally impressed by the PDJ Academy and the facilities. They gave instructive feedback concerning the training methods used and told how they used the key account analysis and strategy project from the course for business purposes or for career development in the company after the course.

These more senior sales people are less dependent on the support from their managers and have less direct contact. This may explain why only 63% of their managers reported that B2B has had either high or moderate impact on the business results.

Fourteen percent of B2B participants reported "little impact." Some seasoned sales people admit that they found it difficult to change their personal style and some were more involved in managerial work than in sales and they were therefore not able to use the sales techniques personally.

Actions After the SCM Study

Recommendations

A nine-day residential course is a major investment and although the study documented a considerable business impact as pay-back it was worth considering if any elements of the training could be removed in order to reduce the course duration and save costs. To ensure that the course is equally relevant for all participants we recommended that the PDJ Academy offer different versions of the CBC course to sales and non-sales staff. In almost every case of low impact, we had noted that the participants were in a role that could not have directly benefited from the course.

Even though 60% of participants report high or moderate impact that they were able to verify, it was worthwhile considering how the amount of high impact could be increased as nearly 20% of participants did not achieve this level of impact. Based on what we learned about factors that enabled or impeded impact we were able to show the importance of involving managers in pre- and post-course activities and planning time and resources for the implementation.

We made a very interesting eye-opening observation in connection with the B2B study. The course contains a so-called "eight-step key account process." According to the survey only a few participants had subsequently used this process and, according to survey data, it did not seem to have any remarkable influence on the volume or the value of sales nor on retaining or acquiring customers. Had we relied only on the survey data, we might have been tempted to recommend that the PDJ Academy take it out of the curriculum. However, the interviews disclosed some very impressive stories about the benefits of the eight-step process from people who had achieved excellent business results. When we dug into the experience through the interviews, some high-success participants reported that they had relied on precisely this tool. So instead we ended up recommending that the PDJ Academy put more emphasis on the eight-step process.

A success rate of more than 80% of B2B participants reporting high or moderate business impact (23% high) strongly supported a recommendation that the PDJ Academy should continue along the same lines with this course. To further support the impact we recommended that the Academy might focus more on the English skills of participants in order to make sure that they are sufficiently fluent in English to participate actively in the course and to make sure it has real business relevance for the people attending. In order to meet the needs of the CBC level we also recommended that national differences in selling styles and management styles be integrated into the training.

Decisions

One to two months later we arranged a public seminar, open to the local training professional public, where the CEO of the PDJ Academy presented the results of the study to an internal and external audience and pointed out the development areas, that they have chosen to focus on as a result of the study. Also, according to the CEO the SCM study clarified questions which had so far not been resolved about the business value of these Academy courses.

As a result of the SCM study the PDJ Academy has taken a number of steps to secure the long-term impact of this and other programs:

They have changed their informal and formal communications to focus on training as more of a process rather than an "event," and they refer specifically to a "learning period" instead of "a course"; this learning period begins before the formal course commences and continues after trainees return to the workplace and begin to implement their new skills.

They have introduced a modified High Impact Learning (as referred to in Brinkerhoff & Apking, 2001) approach to the learning process. For example, training participants are asked to complete an impact model before training and to discuss it with their managers before and after training.

They have developed a learning management concept dealing with the role and the capacity of the local managers to implement the new skills of their employees in the work environment. This new approach provides, for example, a new toolbox for managers and sales staff that contains impact maps (Brinkerhoff & Apking 2001) and other impact-enhancing methods and tools.

They have recruited a consultant whose job it is to support, coach, and keep track of the implementation of the training after the course.

They conduct learning seminars in the regional companies in order to increase the awareness of implementation of learning and to help managers understand and use the implementation tools.

The SCM study is being used to communicate examples of impact and benefits from the training and to create awareness and more of a focus on post-training implementation. The SCM study is also used by sales staff—together with other measurement data—to document to customers the value added by the PDJ Academy to the Grundfos' emphasis on quality.

Lessons Learned

Though my colleagues and I were seasoned evaluation and measurement professionals, this was our first experience with a major SCM study.

We were surprised how much information we got and how useful it was to the PDJ Academy. We realized that the individual stories (impact profiles) contained information "between the lines" which the Academy understood and valued better than we had anticipated.

One of the B2B participants was asked by a journalist how it felt to be measured; was it unpleasant? He replied that it was not at all unpleasant. On the contrary: it reminded him that he could use the training even more, and thus it led to even better results.

Not all people who claimed "high impact" were eligible as "Success Cases." In fact some of the candidates who claimed "moderate" impact had achieved more valuable results. To some extent how people rate and describe their success depends on personality and on cultural differences; a learning application and outcome that one person considers "highly successful' might be considered by another person to be only "moderate," for example. This exposes a weakness with pure quantitative surveys. The interviews were a verification and correction of such differences. Further, we recognized that the timing of a follow-up study is important and that with some practice it is possible to tell relatively soon during an interview whether the story is going to qualify as a viable Success Case instance or not.

In this case we chose to use two people during each interview, which, of course, is time consuming, because of language barriers and difficulties. On the other hand we learned the advantages of telephone interviews. One is that you can take notes and consult your papers more freely than in a face-to-face interview where you must have eye contact and may need to tape-record the interview and, consequently, may have to invest even more time in a transcription of the tape afterwards. Also when you talk on the phone, you can bring the interview to an end in a polite manner after five to ten minutes if the respondent does not have a valid and verifiable success story. That is not quite as easy when you have arranged a personal face-to-face interview.

Verification is crucial for the validity of the study. In this case we were able to get very precise details about the individual performance. In addition, the survey among the managers of the CBC and B2B partici- pants was a verification tool. However, we were not able to document in a SCM framework whether the success criteria from the impact model, "Improve customer satisfaction," had been achieved, as this would have required that we speak with the customer. The learning point then would be to stick to success criteria that can be measured in the context of the study or make sure you have access to supporting data. In this case, however, we were able to make inferences about probable customer satis- faction, as we had gathered verifiable information about sales staff taking actions that were highly likely to increase customer satisfaction, such as making sure that an order was accurate and fulfilled on time.

Chapter Eleven

Service Technician Training at the Compaq Computer Corporation

Carmie Boutin and Cheryl Brogan

*T*his chapter presents and explains the Success Case Method (SCM) study conducted for Compaq Computer Corporation. This case shows how the SCM was applied to assess the impact of a technical training program aimed at preparing field-service technicians to initialize and assure the proper operation of newly-installed communications equipment that would enable clients' computer server systems to interface with other computer system elements and internet communications devices.

This case describes how the SCM was used to gauge the business impact of training and, then, to identify performance system factors that were interfering with broader impact. In short, the case shows how the SCM was used not only to identify and document substantial business impact of the training, but also to discover why a significant proportion of training participants did not fully achieve the expected results, and further, how the causes for this partial lack of impact were isolated and addressed with the SCM.

Other Important Factors

At the time of our study, the company was a major global computer equipment and service provider. The business model was fairly simple, though the organization, because it had grown rapidly through a number of mergers and acquisitions, was fairly complex. Readers, however, need not have a full understanding of all of the organizational complexities in order to understand and learn from this case. The company developed computer products and technology; sold hardware equipment, associated operating and supporting software; and provided service contracts to customers to maintain and upgrade computer installations. The organization in which the evaluation was conducted was a part of the division that both sold large computer server systems to customers, as well as provided service on a contracted basis to maintain the servers and assure their effective and efficient performance to customers. This area of the company was highly important, as it both generated substantial revenues and profits, serving a number of large, high-profile and important customers. Several major airlines, for example, relied on their computer server equipment that enabled their company's reservation system to operate. One of America's largest stock exchanges was another key customer. In short, customers in this division were highly visible and important; they required and expected flawless service.

Technical Services

Service technicians in the technical services area were the learners involved in the training program that was evaluated. The technical services area was a part of the larger field services division that both sold and serviced the large computer server systems and the peripheral equipment needed to make them fully functional. While the field sales portion of the services area reported to a different vice president, field sales and technical services needed to work closely together to retain customers, sell continuous upgrades, and install and maintain customers' equipment.

The technical services area was organized into geographic work units that provided support to customers in their respective geographic territories. Each territory had a managing technical service director and a parallel managing director for sales. Technical service representatives were highly skilled people who could install, set up and initialize, troubleshoot, and maintain all of the various hardware elements and configurations that the company sold to customers. Each technician was assigned to a certain set of customers, and it was their responsibility to keep the customer's systems working well and keep the customers fully satisfied with the service they received from the company. Like any high-tech industry, the company was constantly engaged in research and development. New products and technologies and new upgrades and improvements were constantly being introduced in a high-pressure rush to stay ahead of the competition. This meant that technicians were in constant need of training and re-training, as new equipment and new modalities for existing equipment were introduced to the field.

About the Training

The training in question was a two-week residential course to teach technicians how to install and initialize Maxidata servers—a fictitious name for the company's largest and newest server— and associated hardware and some highly complex peripheral equipment that enabled the server at the customer's site to communicate with other internal server elements and external databases and equipment. Initialization of the hardware boxes was crucial, because without the proper initialization codes and settings they would not operate effectively, or at all.

Initialization was itself a complex process taking a minimum of several hours during which certain parts of the client's server must be shut down temporarily.

The course consisted of technical presentation of complex material and an intensive set of application exercises on a simulator that enabled participating technicians to practice initialization of the various hardware elements and configurations. The simulation portion of the course was vital to success, because this was where the technicians got to practice each of the various and complex initialization procedures. A key portion of the instruction was practice in using a large technical manual, particularly in using the manual as a reference guide to input troubleshooting codes and in interpreting the many different code variations the server could repeat back in response to each test procedure. They would learn how to use the manual and its attendant code procedures, then practice actual setup, initialization , test, and troubleshooting procedures on the simulator, which itself was a large server with ports for all of the various peripheral installations and upgrades.

Importantly, the course was limited in attendance due to the reliance on the simulator to provide practice and skill building. This meant that only a limited number of technicians—usually no more than 16—could take the course at one time, becasue more participants could not effectively use the limited simulator. When we asked why they could not add a simulator, we were told that the cost of the server was prohibitive. Further, the new servers were in such demand in the market that any additional servers would be sold to the growing number of customers on the waiting list. Capacity could not keep up with demand in the market, and any suggestion that the company fail to fill a lucrative and profitable order because "training" needed more capacity was met with outright disbelief. Sales had let the training division know that they were lucky to have the server for use as a simulator at all, and, in fact, there had even been a suggestion that was barely fended off to sell it to a customer. In short, training capacity was limited and would stay limited. We did not know at the time how this factor would play later into our report and how important it would be in shaping the conclusions of our evaluation effort.

The Training Context

Several issues and factors related to the training context are important for understanding the study discussed in this case.

Class availability: As we noted, the course duration was two full weeks. But because the simulator needed to be recalibrated and re-set for the next class, it was not possible to conduct a class every two weeks. This factor and other field service demand and operational cycles conspired to allow only 16 classes to be conducted each year. Thus, there was almost always a waiting list for the class, and it was not unusual for a technician who wanted to register for the class to have to wait several months. Again, we were not aware at the time we planned the evaluation how important this factor would become later in our evaluation.

Registration process: Participants for the course were nominated by their geographic territory manager, who then directed them to complete an application for course attendance. Admission was accomplished on a first-come, first-served basis, except that course administrators would defer admission to any second applicants from the same service territory. Because space was limited, the rationale was that no single territory could use up two seats in the course, if there were others waiting to participate from other service territories. A waiting list was constructed, again based solely on order of applications received. Territory service managers were allocated only a limited training budget and limited access to this and other courses, another fact that would emerge as important later.

Political tensions: The client for the evaluation was the training department in the field services area, the business division that was responsible for providing support services to customers who had purchased the servers. This department paid for the training. It was their budget that supported the training, and if there were problems with the training, they were the first to receive complaints. The field technical services division was the primary customer for the training, as their technicians were the ones who needed the training and who applied the training in the field. The field sales division was a secondary customer, or at least a vitally interested party. If a customer was not satisfied with service, rightly or wrongly, field sales was at risk, as unhappy customers were unlikely to stay on as future customers. Typically, as one might expect, customer expressions of dissatisfaction were blamed on the other division. If service received a complaint, they invariably said it was the fault of sales reps who made unrealistic promises for installation and service or oversold system capabilities. If sales received a complaint, they always said it was service's fault. Whenever a problem really was because of a failure of service, the training department was quick to get the blame, as they were accused of providing inadequate training, inadequate access to training, wrong information, and so forth.

Divided "ownership": Adding spice to this political brew was the fact that, while the training division supported the Maxidata course out of their budget, it was not their program. Rather, the program was "owned" by a separately administered technical support division that had been a part of the previously acquired company and reported to an entirely different part of the complex organization. This division designed the training, hired and managed the training staff, maintained the simulator, and so forth. They felt over-managed and micro-managed by the training division that actually owned the budget. On the other hand, the training department because it was in the same division as the field sales and field support functions, felt all the pressure of making the course successful and delivering results. Criticisms about the course were always leveled at them. But they really had no control over the program and could not influence it other than to manipulate the budget.

Course under fire: In response to complaints from field sales about the "effectiveness" of the course, the training department decided it was time to commission an impartial evaluation. The complaints about course effectiveness were quite general and implied that the course was not sufficient to prepare a fully capable technical support staff in the field. Most complaints had come from field support and sales managers; there were few from course participants themselves. The course "owners" reacted to such complaints defensively and said that if anything was wrong with the course, it was the fact that they could not get enough resources to run it properly. The evaluation was intended to settle the question of whether the course was good enough. Did it work well and serve the business needs it was intended to address? This was the question we were asked to resolve.

Preparing for the Evaluation

To understand the expected goals for the course and to determine exactly how it was intended to address business needs, we conducted brief telephone interviews with the directors of field sales, the director of technical support, and the director of the technical training curriculum who was the course owner. We also discussed the course goals and needs for the evaluation with the directors of training in the office that had commissioned the evaluation—the training department in the support services division. From these talks we determined the nature and objectives of the course (enough so that we understood what the parts of it were and how they were to be applied in service settings). We also analyzed the audience for the course, being sure we understood the numbers of service technicians who were candidates for the course, how many had attended in the past year or so, when the course had been conducted, and so forth.

Based on these discussions, we decided to include in the evaluation all of the service technicians who had completed the course in the past ten months. This number was chosen for two primary reasons. First, this would go back in time far enough so that we had a reasonably large number of participants who had completed the course, from 12 classes totaling 172 participants. This number gave us service technicians from all of the major geographic service areas, including Europe, South America, Australia, and the Pacific Basin. We also felt that it went far enough back in time that it would allow sufficient time for application of course-acquired skills, as the most recent class completing the course was two months prior to our commencement of the evaluation. Second, the ten-month window took us back in time to when there had been a major revision to the course. The course administrators explained that just previous to that time, they had made a change, adding considerably more simulator practice on an upgraded simulator, and also some performance tools, specifically a CD-ROM disk of the reference manual that participants could access on a laptop computer. Finally, we felt that we were not going so far back in time that the experience of the course and any application from it would be lost from participants' memories.

The Impact Model

Based on our discussions with the several stakeholders, particularly the course owners and the manager of technical support, we created and confirmed the impact model. This impact model is presented below in Table 11-1.

Table 11-1 Impact Model for Maxidata Server Technical Support Training

Key Skills and Knowledge	Critical Applications	Key Results	Business Impact
Understand competitive advantage of Maxidata servers	Initialize Maxidata servers	All Maxidata equipment correctly initialized, operating effectively, and ready to fulfill customer processing requirements	Customer systems fully functional and error-free
Understand functionality and capabilities of Maxidata server peripherals	Install and initialize Maxidata peripherals		
Be able to initialize a newly installed Maxidata server	Test server integration to identify and repair any operating problems		Complete customer satisfaction
Be able to install and initialize and test Maxidata peripherals			
Be able to test integrated operation of the server and peripherals and troubleshoot initialization problems			

Readers will note that the impact model in this case is very simple, despite the complexity and technical nature of the training. The content of the course was, obviously, highly technical and complex. But, for purposes of a Success Case evaluation, there was no need for us to have an in-depth understanding of the course content. We needed to know, for example, the general structure of the two-week session so that, if interview respondents mentioned some part of the training, we would recognize it correctly. We also needed to understand how the course skills would be applied, and, because this involved technical applications, we took time to be sure that we knew the names of the several products involved (the Maxidata server, and the several pieces of peripheral equipment). We further wanted to know what general function each piece served. Thus, for example, we knew that a "DUCK box" (a name for one of the pieces of peripheral equipment) was a communications "box" that helped connect the server to new telecommunications equipment. This was enough for us to be able to participate in an interview and recognize the different applications of training content to which an interviewee might refer.

Planning the Survey

Names and e-mail addresses of all participants who had completed the course in the past 12 months were readily available. With so few training application opportunities, there was no need for a long list of training application items. Further, there was a good deal of demographic information available that was keyed to the names of the technical service reps who were the course participants. Thus, given a participant name, we could immediately discover the customers served by that service rep, the geographic region, and so forth. All of this combined to allow a very brief survey instrument—administered by e-mail—which is shown in its entirety in Figure 11-1.

Greetings!

You are receiving this message because you completed the Maxidata M-Series Communications Products course this calendar year. Services Training and Development is working in collaboration with Compaq EC to evaluate the effectiveness of this course.

Please take a few moments to answer these questions. Please note that any responses are held in strict confidence. Your input is valuable and will help make the training more effective.

(continued)

Please respond no later than August 5, 2000, and send your responses to alexandre.putinski@maxipaq.com.

Question 1: Have you had at least one opportunity in providing service to a Maxidata customer to apply any of the learning you acquired in the Maxidata M-Series Communications Products training in a service opportunity?

YES or NO

If YES, go to Question 2.

If NO, please return your survey now to alexandre.putinski@maxipaq.com

Question 2: Choose the most helpful and valuable instance in which you applied the Maxidata training. (If there was only one instance, refer to that instance.) How successful was the outcome of the service you provided?

1—Service was not at all successful

2—Service was between "not at all successful" and "adequate"

3—Service was adequate

4—Service was between "adequate" and "very successful"

5—Service was very successful

Question 3: Have you applied your Maxidata training in more than one customer service instance? If NO, skip this question and return your survey now. If YES, choose the response below that best summarizes the outcomes of all of these instances together:

1. None of the rest of them was anywhere near as successful as the instance reflected in Question 2

2. Some were as successful as in Question 2, but most were not

3. About half were as successful as in Question 2

4. Most were as successful as in Question 2

5. All were as successful as in Question 2

(continued)

Thank you. Please return your survey now by reply mail or to alexandre.putinski@compaq.com.

Alexandre Putinski

Information & Performance Solutions

446-256-8805 (phone)

446-256-8483 (fax)

Figure 11-1   Evaluation: E-Mail Survey Message

Evaluation Results

Surveys were e-mailed to all 172 participants who had completed the course in the past ten-month period that was agreed would be the focus of the evaluation. Of the participants, 74% or 127 returned a completed e-mail survey. In order to test for a possible response bias, a random sample (12 participants) of those 45 participants who did not respond to the initial e-mail request was surveyed by telephone. Of the 127 respondents, 77 (61%) indicated that they had made at least one application of the Maxidata course teachings in a customer service situation. Surprisingly, of all the respondents, 50 (39%) indicated that they had made no use at all of the Maxidata course learning since completing the course.

These results are summarized in Table 11-2.

Table 11-2 Application of Maxidata Course Learning in a Customer Service Setting

Survey Item	Result
Proportion of course participants who completed the survey	74% (127 of 172)
Participants who reported at least one application of the training	61% (77 of 127)
Participants who reported no application of the training in any customer service situation	50 (39% of 127)

Possible Survey Response Rate Bias

In SCM studies, it is common to find more learning users responding to the survey while non-respondents tend to be those with little or no learning application. Follow-up calls to those who did not respond to the initial e-mail survey confirmed this tendency. The calls to the random sample of 12 non-respondents to the survey found only one more person who reported usage of the training, and the outcome of that one instance was rated by the service rep as less than fully successful. This led us to believe that the population of non-respondents was more than likely to represent service reps that did not make much, if any, successful use of their training. While we did not literally add all of these numbers into the reported non-users, we did feel very comfortable in reporting that the 39% who did not use the training at all was probably an underestimate, and that the actual proportion of trainees who made no use of the training was greater than 40%. For purposes of more simple and clear communication, we reported a non-use estimate of 40% in the remainder of our reporting documents and activities.

Outcomes of Service Applications

Readers will recall that the survey shown in Figure 11-1 asked respondents to rate the outcomes of the service they provided using their Maxidata training. The responses were so overwhelmingly positive that we suspected a possible bias in reporting. But the telephone interviews confirmed that the service technicians who used their training were able to do so with great success; we could not find any substantial differences in the nature and value of the service outcomes achieved among those respondents who reported "adequate" outcomes, those who reported "very successful" outcomes, and those who reported something in between these choices. This led us to believe that the differences in the response choices selected reflected more about the relative size and value of the customer account and the value the service technician placed on the account (or perhaps the modesty, or lack of modesty of the service rep) than the value of the outcome to the customer. There was no doubt from the findings that the training, when it was applied, was applied successfully and with satisfaction to the customer.

Another question (the third and last survey item) asked essentially how unique the service outcome reported in Question 2 had been. That is, we wondered if service technicians were able to apply their learning only some of the time with success, or if their applications (when there were more than one) were leading to consistent outcomes in all service instances...

Respondents in the interviews were very firm in expressing their belief that the training, when they used it, helped them achieve the outcomes their customers needed. This was a very positive result in our eyes and in the view of our client. But, readers should remember that such results were claimed for only 60% of the respondents. And, given that we did not hear from some participants, it is was very likely that this 60% estimate was exaggerated.

In sum, it was quite clear that the training was working well when it was being used, but that there was a large proportion of the trainees who were making no use of their training at all. The cost of training all of these non-users was in the hundreds of thousands of dollars, none of which had any pay off. Given the pressure to serve customers and save money in a market of declining profits, why, we wondered, would people go through training such as this and then not use it—not even once? If we had this question, readers can be certain that management was even more concerned.

The Rest of the Story

Our interviews of the non-users (non-Success Cases) quickly cleared up the mystery. The explanation was vividly simple, though quite unreasonable. Technicians who did not use their skills reported that they had no customers—none, zero—who had purchased the DUCK box peripherals, and, thus, there was no need nor was there an opportunity for them to apply the course skills; what the course taught was how to initialize equipment which none of their customers owned! The next question was, of course, "Then why did you attend the course?" The answer to this, which sometimes we had to get from interviews of district managers, was the following:

Sales projections were viewed as unreliable, so even though no customer was scheduled for a DUCK box sale and installation, district managers wanted someone on their staff to be ready with the DUCK box skills, just in case. Further, district managers knew there was a waiting list for the course, so they placed a technician on the list to attend, to assure a placement, again, just in case they had a need because of a customer purchase. The waiting list was long, of course, partly because so many technicians who did not really need the course were taking it anyway. This was made worse by some technicians re-enrolling for the course, because when they first took it they had no customer with the product, but now when they did have a customer, it had been so long since they took the course that they needed it again.

In sum, the course was highly effective. It taught the skills and taught them well. When the skills were needed, virtually every technician was able to fulfill customer expectations. We uncovered and documented Success Case after Success Case where a trained technician "saved the day" by quickly solving a problem that, had it not been solved, would have led to a disastrous customer outage. In one Success Case, a technician was confronted by 30 inoperable DUCK boxes. The customer was the large American stock exchange. Had the outage gone even minutes longer than scheduled (service was temporarily transferred to an airline's server), the entire stock exchange would have crashed causing millions of dollars in losses. But, the technician recalled from the training knew exactly how to look up the trouble codes. They discovered a coding error in the delivered equipment, made quick diagnoses and repairs, and got the server working before a crash could occur. Inquiry during this interview showed that there was no doubt that the training was a critical and necessary component of this highly successful service instance.

Clearly, the course was fine as it was and was contributing to a very positive ROI when we compared the worth of outcomes achieved to the costs of maintaining and implementing the course. But, the 40% non-use rate was seriously undermining the cost-effectiveness of the course, making it far more expensive on a per-result basis than it should have been. Worse, the troublesome practice of enrolling people who could not use the course was causing a severe backlog, risking that a person who needed it would not get it, thus leading to a potential customer outage or complaints, which the company knew in turn led to a loss of a customer and long-term revenue source.

Though it took several months of discussion back and forth between divisions and factions, we were finally able to convene a phone conference among the senior players in the divisions affected and discuss the findings and conclusions. They reached a decision to redesign and tighten up enrollment procedures to reduce enrollments such that only those technicians who had a true need (for example, a reliably projected customer that would need service) could get access to the course. There was some business value, of course, for some degree of over-training, as this would assure that the "just in case" scenario would not lead to an un-served customer. To address this issue, they agreed that, in the event a service area had a customer with the DUCK boxes, but no trained technician, then a trained technician could be used on loan from another district with no loss of incentive or bonus pay or any other such financial penalty to either district involved.

The final result of this SCM project was that the client gained a large increase in the ROI of a training investment, which in turn led to a greater assurance of effective customer service; all without changing any aspect of a training program itself. When viewed from the perspective of the larger learning-performance system, of course, the "training" program had some serious flaws. But it took a more systemic inquiry to uncover these and get the right information to the right people.

Chapter Twelve

Coaching and Training at Coffee Bean and Tea Leaf®

Scott Blanchard and Dennis Dressler

T he Coffee Bean and Tea Leaf® is a chain of coffee shops located in the Southern California and Phoenix, Arizona, areas. When the training in this scenario was offered, the company had just over 100 retail outlets. The company originated in 1963 and grew somewhat slowly during its early history. It was one of the earliest "coffee shop" chains, starting well before the current coffee shop chain phenomenon in the United States. The company, however, has undergone very rapid growth in the past several years.

The company utilizes a fully integrated operational model. It purchases coffees beans and tea leaves globally, blends, flavors, and roasts those products in a Southern California processing operation, and makes fresh baked products and sandwiches in a commissary operation to provide the retail stores. (Because the current Arizona operation is a new, expansion market, baked goods and sandwiches are produced under contract in that area.)

The management structure of the company is quite typical. The company has the usual corporate support staff roles (finance, human resources, purchasing, and so forth) and a system of regional, district, and local store management for its retail operations. Roasting and food production also has its own management structure and leadership but that also is fairly traditional. Each retail store has a general manager, one or more assistant general managers, several shift supervisors, and a large number of baristas, mostly part time employees. Each store will employ a total of 30 to 40 staff.

The Business Scenario

Coffee Bean and Tea Leaf had moved to a rapid growth strategy, planning to grow from more than 100 retail outlets in 2004 to 150 outlets in 2005. The company was rightfully concerned about its ability to develop or hire enough capable general managers to effectively fuel their retail store growth strategy. Given this concern, the company contacted the Ken Blanchard companies to discuss general manager development issues.

When Blanchard's consultants met with the company to more fully understand the leadership development need, they discovered that not only was developing general managers for 50 new retail stores critical, but in 2003, 50 of their current general managers had left the company. This meant that if the company stayed at the same general manager attrition levels in 2004 and added 50 new retail stores in 2005, the actual number of new general managers needed was approximately 100 in the next year. These facts convinced both the Coffee Bean and Tea Leaf and the Blanchard companies that this initiative needed to develop new general managers and retain those that were currently effective in order for the company to achieve its growth goals. It also made very clear what the measurable outcome needed to be—retain and grow general managers.

Jointly, the Blanchard and Coffee Bean and Tea Leaf companies elected to have their current management staff, in all areas of the company, participate in Blanchard's Situational Leadership IIR leadership development course followed by ten individual coaching sessions for each manager. These coaching sessions were provided by professionally trained and certified coaches from Coaching.com, the coaching arm of The Ken Blanchard Companies.

The Training Intervention

Prior to anyone starting the Situational Leadership IIR course, all managers were provided with an impact map, a specialized tool (see Advantage Performance, 2005) that defines and clarifies a "line of sight" between intended learning outcomes, on-the-job learning applications and results, and the business goals to which these learning applications and results are meant to contribute. This map visually demonstrated the linkage between the Situational Leadership IIR (SLIIR) course learning and individual coaching, critical leader tasks and outcomes, and their contribution to the achievement of the Coffee Bean and Tea Leaf strategic goals. All training and coaching participants and their manager were provided with a guide to help them engage in a dialogue about the impact map, what specific leadership tasks and outcomes were unique to their leadership position, and how the training and coaching could help deliver personal and company value.

The Blanchard facilitator of the Situational Leadership IIR course also used the participants' impact maps throughout the actual training. These "map re-visit" portions of the training helped participants stay focused on their purpose and application of the training and helped them see links between learning, their personal accountability, and the company's goals. The individual coaches also used the impact maps to guide the coaching discussions and application assignment and activities.

Participants completed, over a two-week period, an electronically delivered version of the knowledge content portion of the Situational Leadership IIR course. Then participants gathered for the skill practice portion of the course. The ten coaching sessions then followed the skill practice portion; participants were encouraged to have one coaching session every two weeks. These sessions were telephone facilitated and lasted 45 to 60 minutes each. All sessions were focused on applying what had been learned in the course in ways that would make measurable differences to the Coffee Bean and Tea Leaf business goals, leveraging the impact mapping dialogue that already occurred.

This entire initiative was launched in early 2004 with 49 manager participants from the Coffee Bean and Tea Leaf company. The last of the coaching sessions was completed in late summer of 2004. This Success Case study was initiated in February 2005 and was completed in March 2005.

The Evaluation Purpose

The purpose of this Success Case Method (SCM) study was to help the Coffee Bean and Tea Leaf company determine whether it should roll out the same initiative to its store general managers and possibly to promising assistant general managers. In addition, The Ken Blanchard Companies co-sponsored this study because it was very interested in knowing whether this implementation of the Situational Leadership IIR course and the follow-up coaching using impact maps and manager/participant dialogue produced significant business impact.

Staff from the Learning Alliance completed all professional evaluation services. Both the Blanchard and Coffee Bean and Tea Leaf companies provided project administrative and support services, but were not directly involved in evaluation data gathering. All parties agreed that this was essential to help make the study more objective and confidential.

The project faced a constraint that is quite common with a Success Case Method (SCM) study—namely, getting very busy leaders to take a few minutes to complete a survey and for just a few of those leaders to participate in a short telephone interview. For this study at Coffee Bean and Tea Leaf, these obstacles existed but did not become a barrier to gathering quality impact data. It simply took about a week longer than anticipated to complete the Success Case interviews.

SCM Study Procedures

The Learning Alliance and Blanchard team met with the client and confirmed the business outcomes at which the training and coaching was aimed. These had already been discussed, of course, as these were the impetus for the training in the first place. Thus, this step in the SCM process was accomplished quite quickly and involved little client time and virtually no debate.

The survey used in this study is shown in its entirety on the next page as Figure 12-1. This survey was constructed as a web-posted tool, thus the instructions direct respondents to identify their item choices by clicking on a radio button.

As a result of what you learned in the Situational Leadership IIR course and the coaching that followed it, you may have applied your learning in the following ways. You may also have had a range of successes in that application. Review the possibilities and then select the radio button that most closely matches your results after trying the application listed.

Application Possibility	I have tried this and it has produced positive results.	I have tried this but I am not sure yet what will result.	I have not tried this but I have plans to do so.	I have not tried this and have no plans to do so.
Set clear performance goals and expectations for/with others	O	O	O	O
Used actions and opportunities to develop the competence and commitment of others	O	O	O	O
Provided flexible leadership consistent with what others needed from me in order to grow and be successful	O	O	O	O
Used coaching and individual work sessions to focus on development needs and agenda of the other person	O	O	O	O

(continued)

Application Possibility	I have tried this and it has produced positive results.	I have tried this but I am not sure yet what will result.	I have not tried this but I have plans to do so.	I have not tried this and have no plans to do so.
Took action to develop my own competence and commitment for the success of self, others, and the company	O	O	O	O

Applications of Situational Leadership IIR learning and coaching might lead to a range of outcomes. From the list below, select the statements that best represent any outcomes you believe your learning applications may have helped produce.

O   Retained a high potential Coffee Bean Team Member

O   Developed someone for a more responsible, challenging leadership position

O   Helped a marginal performing Team Member become a high-performing Team Member

O   Helped someone or a store achieve important operational goals

O   None of the above but something else very important

O   Cannot say that the Situational Leadership IIR course and the coaching has produced any valuable outcomes

(continued)

When someone participates in company-provided training and coaching, there can be a range of reactions to the value of that training. Rate how valuable you found the experience.

O   I found it very valuable and it has helped produce very positive, concrete business impact.

O   I found it very valuable but I cannot say that it has helped produce business impact yet.

O   I found it very valuable at a personal level but I do not think it will really help the business.

O   I already knew and was doing everything I learned in this process so it was of little value.

O   I found the process largely a waste of time and resources.

Name ——————————————————————————————

(Your survey feedback only goes to the Learning Alliance, our partner for this project. They need your name in case they would like to ask you some follow up questions to better understand your experience. Your survey data and name will not be shared with anyone at Coffee Bean and Tea Leaf.

Figure 12-1 Coffee Bean and Tea Leaf ®—Success Case Method Survey

After the survey was reviewed and approved by Coffee Bean and Tea Leaf and Ken Blanchard stakeholders, it was programmed into a public, Web-based survey software called Zoomerang. Once it was posted on the Zoomerang Web site it was tested with several internal Coffee Bean and Tea Leaf staff members. This was a vital step, as the Learning Alliance evaluation team had to be sure that the survey could be accessed by company managers and that their responses would be accurately and thoroughly recorded. Sometimes, company computer and e-mail security procedures will interfere with accessing externally posted surveys, but this field trial showed that there were no problems.

Once the survey was posted and known to work, the evaluation team implemented the following steps to complete the SCM evaluation.

1. Drafted a message to be signed by a senior Coffee Bean and Tea Leaf executive. This message explained the evaluation purpose and process and asked managers to cooperate by responding to the survey. The message included the URL address of the Web-based survey and was sent to all targeted participants by the Coffee Bean and Tea Leaf sponsor.

2. Monitored survey responses and provided assistance in sending follow-up messages to non-respondents.

3. Analyzed all survey responses and selected in-depth interview candidates from amongst those who appeared to be in the "high success" and "low success" categories.

4. Sent the selected interview candidates an e-mail message asking them to schedule a telephone interview time with the evaluators.

5. Completed the in-depth phone interviews along with detailed interview notes with each interview candidate.

6. Analyzed all survey and interview data and arrived at findings, impact profiles, and recommendations.

7. Wrote a detailed impact study report containing the items mentioned in step 1 plus sections on the introduction, study methodology, and an appendix that contained the impact maps, the survey, all survey data, and the interview protocol.

8. Asked for feedback and comments on the report from key Coffee Bean and Tea Leaf and Blanchard stakeholders.

9. Finalized the report and used it to create a three-page executive summary of the report.

10. Provided these finalized items to key Coffee Bean and Tea Leaf and Blanchard stakeholders, and offered to discuss any study outcomes with anyone at Coffee Bean and Tea Leaf and Blanchard companies.

Survey Results

Of the 49 initiative participants sent the survey, 33 returned completed surveys, a return rate of more than 67%.

Survey results are shown in Table 12-1, presenting the frequency and percentage of responses for each of the survey items.

Table 12-1 Survey Responses

Application Possibility	I have tried this and it has produced positive results.	I have tried this but I am not sure yet what will result.	I have not tried this but I have plans to do so.	I have not tried this and have no plans to do so.
Set clear performance goals and expectations for/with others	O	O	O	O
Used actions and opportunities to develop the competence and commitment of others	O	O	O	O
Provided flexible leadership consistent with what others needed from me in order to grow and be successful	O	O	O	O

(continued)

Table 12-1 Survey Responses (Continued)

Application Possibility	I have tried this and it has produced positive results.	I have tried this but I am not sure yet what will result.	I have not tried this but I have plans to do so.	I have not tried this and have no plans to do so.
Used coaching and individual work sessions to focus on development needs and agenda of the other person	O	O	O	O
Took action to develop my own competence and commitment for the success of self, others, and the company	O	O	O	O

Outcomes contributed to by applications of learning:

O   Retained a high potential Coffee Bean Team Member

N = 8 or 24%

O   Developed someone for a more responsible, challenging leadership position

N = 22 or 67%

O   Helped a marginal performing Team Member become a high performing Team Member

N = 21 or 64%

O   None of the above but something else very important

N = 6 or 18%

O   I cannot say that the Situational Leadership IIR course and the coaching has produced any valuable outcomes

N = 1 or 3%

Reactions to the Value of the Training

O   I found it very valuable and it has helped produce very positive, concrete business impact.

N = 21 or 68%

O   I found it very valuable but I cannot say that it has helped produce business impact yet.

N = 9 or 29%

O   I found it very valuable at a personal level but I do not think it will really help the business.

N = 0 or 0%

O   I already knew and was doing everything I learned in this process so it was of little value.

N = 1 or 3%

O   I found the process largely a waste of time and resources.

N = 0 or 0%

As can be seen, the survey data summary reveals a very high reported level of learning application and subsequent results achieved. A clear majority of respondents on virtually all items reported positive applications of learning and subsequent business results.

Using only these survey results, it might be tempting to conclude that this initiative had very positive business impact. The interviews in this SCM are specifically structured to either confirm these survey outcomes or discover what caused these data to look as positive as they do. The evaluators are presented with several "rival" hypotheses about the outcomes. Each of these was probed and tested during the in-depth interview phase of this study. These potential alternative explanations for the findings, or rival hypotheses, are listed below.

Rival hypothesis 1: The survey data has a strong positive bias and therefore dramatically misrepresents the actual impact. Respondents may not have truthfully reported their post-training experience, simply wanting to say positive things about it for any number of possible reasons.

Rival hypothesis 2: Respondents dramatically overstated the impact of the initiative because they did not fully understand what positive business impact implied and, therefore, claimed positive, concrete business impact without really understanding what that claim meant.

Rival hypothesis 3: There are a lot more "low-impact" initiative participants but they simply chose not to complete the survey.

Another key question the evaluators had to answer was, "Of those who indicated that the initiative was valuable but had not yet seen possible results (nine survey respondents), are they really on the way to positive impact or are they more likely to be 'low-success' participants?"

The rival hypotheses and the question of the true disposition of the non-respondents became key drivers for the in-depth interview portion of this study, in addition to documenting any truly "stand-up-in-court" accounts of individuals using their learning in ways that produced business impact. The evaluators randomly selected six individuals to interview from among those who reported the "highest" levels of impact. Three individuals were randomly selected from among those who reported a valuable experience but "no business impact yet." The lone "low-impact" respondent was also interviewed.

In addition, the evaluators randomly selected six individuals from among the survey non-respondents for an interview. This last group was asked essentially only one question: "Based on your participation in the Situational Leadership IIR and coaching processes, how much impact will your use of what you learned make to Coffee Bean and Tea Leaf's business goals?" The optional answers provided were: "High impact,"

"Modest Impact," "Little Impact," and "No Impact." The purpose of this single question was simply to place these initial non-respondents into a category, determining whether they fall on the "high impact" or the "low or no impact" side of the distribution of all training participants. Then, the evaluators compared the distribution of high versus low impact among the non-respondents to the distribution among the actual respondents to determine if there was a bias.

Interview Results

Based on the telephone interviews, the evaluators uncovered the following:

1. Only one of the six "high-success" cases interviewed proved to be a "false positive." The remaining five interviewees had compelling accounts of how they had used something they learned during the training/coaching process to improve a critical business goal. From this, we concluded that we would need to reduce the overall "high" impact percentage estimate derived from the survey findings alone by one-sixth to account for the one false positive out of the six that were interviewed.

2. Of the three interviewees conducted from the "no results yet" category, we discovered that two of them, in fact, were headed in the direction of producing positive outcomes, while the third interviewee could not describe any intermediate actions and milestones achieved on the way to an important business goal.

3. The one "low" impact participant was interviewed. It was discovered that he had begrudgingly attended the training sessions and did not participate in any coaching sessions. This individual went on to claim that he already knew everything the training taught and was already getting all the coaching he needed from his manager. In following up there was little the evaluators could learn from this

person that was helpful in making suggestions for improving the training; it appeared that the strong and "know it all" attitude of this participant was unlikely to change with any sort of training.

4. The six interviews completed among the random sample of the survey non-respondent group showed that these were essentially no different from the population of survey respondents. That is, four of the six indicated that the initiative had "high" impact while the other two indicated that the initiative had only "modest" impact. Based on these interviews, the evaluators concluded that there was probably no sample bias at work and that the group of non-respondents had experienced about the same levels of learning application and accomplishment of results as those who responded to the initial and larger survey.

After completing the interviews, the evaluators were convinced that this initiative had indeed led to significant business impact. The following is an illustrative story of learning applications and impact derived from the interview phase.

One district manager worked very closely with one of her general managers whose store was underperforming. This general manager was discouraged about this performance and was on the verge of leaving the company. The timing of the district manager's training was fortunate as she finished her training and early coaching sessions in September 2004, coincident with the latest performance reports from the underperforming store and the expressed discouragement of the store manager. Based on this confluence of events, she decided to use her learning to try turning this general manager and store around.

The district manager discovered during the self-analysis portions of the training and coaching sessions that she was very much a "hands-off" manager, believing that if people needed support, they would seek it. In her subsequent application of her learning from the training session, she concluded that this general manager needed a very high level of direction, close and frequent follow-up, and clearer goals and account-ability. At the time of the interview, the district manager reported (and the general manager confirmed) that the store's sales revenues have consistently been up over 50% in weekly sales from the same weeks in the previous year. This run rate projects to a total store and company revenue increase of more than $200,000 annually. Further, the improved direction from the district manager and the subsequent improved success of the store's performance have led to a turn-around in the attitude of the general manager who has now decided to stay the course. The company estimates that bringing on a new general manager costs the company in excess of $75,000 in hiring, training, and "getting up to speed" costs. In sum, this particular application of training led to dramatically increased store revenues and the retention of a seasoned general manager—both key elements of the company's growth strategy.

The evaluators asked this district manager if these results would have been possible without the use of what she had learned in the training and from her coach. She said, "Without the training, this general man-ager would have left the company by now, and I would have a new GM in that store, probably struggling like the former GM. Using the develop-mental model I learned and working with my coach to set clear goals and accountabilities with this GM, positive things have happened. I would not have seen this change without the course and coaching."

The remaining "Success Cases" reported equally substantial and com-pelling accounts of using their training and coaching to produce impact. Based on the economic impact uncovered during this study, the return on investment for the Coffee Bean and Tea Leaf is estimated to be at least three dollars earned for each dollar invested. Over the course of time, this ROI figure will grow even larger as the entire management team embraces and consistently uses a developmental approach to people and performance.

Recommendations

In this case, there was already a very high level of success from the combined training and coaching initiative. Given this, dramatic recommendations that would involve substantial changes were not made, as it was evident that the thoughtfully crafted approach that combined initial impact mapping dialogues with training and sustained coaching was working extremely well.

The evaluators made the following recommendations to Coffee Bean and Tea Leaf:

1. Continue using the Situational Leadership IIR training followed by individual coaching with new managers, and roll it out to the store general manager and assistant general manager positions. This overall recommendation contained these caveats:

    • Assure greater engagement and support of all managers of participants in this training/coaching to further enhance and assure impact.

    • Make sure that all participants have very clear application goals for the learning/coaching before they begin the process, using the impact map and manager dialogue processes to define and clarify these expectations.

2. Provide simple follow up reinforcement resources and communication to make sure the initiative has a high level of sustainability. These reinforcement activities might include simple best practice examples shared in company newsletters and staff meetings, quick e-mail reminders about application opportunities, district and regional retail leader meetings to reinforce the learning and development focus, and quarterly lunch meetings for people to share ideas, barriers, and successes.

3. Apply the implementation method used in this initiative to other company-provided learning (for example, impact maps, manager engagement and dialogue, training experience, coaching for application, impact evaluation). The method has certainly delivered outstanding results in this situation.

Coffee Bean and Tea Leaf has already implemented a number of follow-up and reinforcement activities. In addition, they are working with The Ken Blanchard Companies to design the most impactful process possible for engaging general managers and assistant general managers in a similar initiative. The company has also committed to making sure that all learning initiatives are launched using impact maps and continually educating and asking for manager engagement and support when their direct reports participate in developmental activities.

Challenges and Lessons Learned

During the course of this study, the evaluators found it challenging to schedule interviews with "Success Case" candidates, especially those who were in retail store leadership positions. But, after two short e-mail messages from the senior vice president of human resources, all interviews were successfully scheduled and completed. This reinforced for us the fact that a Success Case method study requires support from senior leadership in order to accomplish the evaluation goals.

Another challenge the evaluators faced in this study was the very small number (one) of "low-success" cases. This single interview did not yield rich data and since it was only one person's experience, the evaluators are not sure if it is strictly an opinion; we have no further evidence that this person's experience was shared by others. Thus, in terms of rich improvement recommendations, the evaluators were rather limited. At the same time, if there are very few "low" successes in the study, and the evaluators have no data showing otherwise, this also speaks to the initiative being well planned and implemented. This outcome is the exception in most impact studies.

In summary, this impact study not only provided rich data to Coffee Bean and Tea Leaf and The Ken Blanchard Companies about the value of this initiative and its implementation method, but also provided clear decision data about providing this experience to general managers and assistant general managers in the company.

Chapter Thirteen

Executive Development at Allstate Insurance

Debbie Kuby and Tim Mooney

*L*ike most companies today, Allstate is faced with the challenge of trying to provide learning and development to a large employee population while operating with finite resources. Because learning and development budgets are limited, learning and development investments must be strategically made to ensure that the expenditures yield business results that support organizational goals and strategies.

One critical area for Allstate is leadership development. As baby boomers in the employee population approach retirement, and as it becomes increasingly difficult to hire top leadership talent from the outside, Allstate HR Education has focused on developing new leaders and enhancing the leadership and business skills of current high-potential managers.

One of the important development programs for leaders is the Allstate Business Simulation (ABS). The Allstate Business Simulation is a two-month executive development program that gives high potential leaders the opportunity to:

• Use strategic planning and fact-based decision-making skills;

• Run a 100 million dollar company through the use of a computer-based simulation;

• Make marketing, finance, human resources, and operations decisions;

• Create an action plan for an Allstate project that links to a strategic goal; and

• Network with key business leaders.

The course is designed to give the managers exposure to business issues and challenges beyond their immediate functional area. It addresses many of the topics covered in most MBA curricula. The course is for high-potential managers and directors with at least five years of experience with Allstate, and requires nomination by an officer to participate.

Evaluation Purposes

This comprehensive course was a significant investment of time and money for the organization. It made good business sense to get answers to the following questions:

Should Allstate continue to offer this comprehensive, yet relatively expensive course?

• If so, how often?

• How are managers using the knowledge they acquired from the development experience?

• What results have they been able to produce?

• How has this benefited them?

- How has this benefited Allstate?
- Is any fine-tuning required to maximize the business impact from the course?

In addition to conducting the evaluation on the ABS, Allstate was also interested in building the capabilities within the organization to conduct future evaluations. Robert Brinkerhoff and Tim Mooney conducted a one-day training session for 12 Allstate employees in human resources education and a few other business unit education areas. This session provided them with a broad understanding of the High Impact Learning SystemsR (HILSR) and the Success Case Evaluation MethodSM. After the training, a smaller team of four human resources education professionals was selected to conduct the evaluation of the ABS using the SCM.

In staffing the team, Allstate wanted to make sure that multiple people were getting the first-hand opportunity to conduct a Success Case Method study. At the same time, they were balancing the inherent challenges associated with having too many people on the team and such a fragmentation of work that no one truly understood the entire process.

The Evaluation Process

Step 1: Determine When to Conduct the Success Case Evaluation

We decided to evaluate the results of the first of two groups of participants that had completed the ABS six months earlier. In addition to the classroom work and computer simulation that were part of the course, participants were asked to create an action plan that they would implement when they were back on their jobs. This would provide them with the opportunity to apply the concepts, processes, and tools they had learned in the ABS. These projects focused on important business issues that Allstate was facing and they varied depending upon the department in which the participants worked. The participants would have had the opportunity to either complete or have made significant progress on their ABS course action plan project.

Step 2: Define Success

Defining "success" in the ABS was a bit more challenging than for many other training programs. First, the course covered a broad range of topics over a period of eight weeks that are traditionally covered in a MBA program (for example, strategy development, finance, operations, human resources, and marketing). Second, the learning objectives of the course are more strategic and knowledge-based than skill-based. Therefore, there was not a narrow set of skills (for instance, how to use a sales process; how to conduct a performance review; or how to apply actuarial methods) that participants were expected to successfully apply on the job. Finally, participants came from various business units and regions across the enterprise. How they would use the principles and strategies would vary depending on which departments they worked in and what their specific roles were.

"Success" was defined broadly but required two components:

1. Participants would be using the knowledge or skills learned in the course to make better decisions back on the job; and as a result,

2. Allstate would realize either revenue generation or cost avoidance.

Another important element of this step was to identify the various stakeholders to whom the evaluation team would report their findings. This was important to ensure that the data that was collected and how it was collected would address the various issues and questions that these stakeholders may have had.

Step 3: Design Survey for all Participants to Search for Best and Worst Cases

A brief on-line survey was designed that was intended to assess the following dimensions:

• Did they complete an action plan (for an action learning project) and were they working on it?

• Were they using information they learned in the training?

• Had they been able to produce a tangible result by applying the learning?

The complete survey is contained in Figure 13-1.

---

1. Some people who participated in the Allstate Business Simulation may have created an action plan. Please select the statement that best represents your current situation:

   O I created an action plan and have fully executed it.

   O I created an action plan and have partially executed it.

   O I created an action plan but have not yet executed any of it.

   O I did not create an action plan, but I intend to.

   O I did not create an action plan and have no plans to do so.

2. Which statement below best represents any action you have taken since your participation in the Allstate Business Simulation?

   O I have implemented something I learned and have achieved a valuable business result (for example, a cost savings, a revenue increase, an improvement in a service or process).

   O I have implemented something I learned and have achieved measurable progress and achieved some key milestones, but it is too early to report any business result yet.

   (continued)

O   I have started to implement some learning, but can't report any interim progress results yet.

O   I have some plans to apply my learning, and though I haven't been able to implement them yet, I fully plan to.

O   For one reason or another (for instance, other priorities, a change in plans) it is unlikely that I will be able to apply any of my learning.

3. In general, how would you characterize the value of this learning experience for you? (Please indicate the statement that best represents your opinion.)

O   I am using one or more of the things I learned in this program, and it is helping me produce what I consider to be a highly valuable result for our business (increased revenues, decreased costs, improved services or processes).

O   I am using one or more of the things I learned in this program, and it is helping me produce what I consider to be a moderately valuable result for our business (increased revenues, decreased costs, improved services and processes).

O   I am using one or more of the things I learned, and I feel they are helping me, but I can't report a specific and concrete result (increased revenues, decreased costs, improved services or processes).

O   I learned some helpful things in the program, and while I may use them in the future, I have not had a chance to do so yet.

O   I found the program interesting, but I don't really see myself making use of it.

Figure 13-1 On-Line Survey

Step 4: Interview Participants and Document Success Cases

Step 4 involved interviewing course participants and documenting Success Cases. Based on the survey results, 34 participants were selected to be interviewed, as follows:

- All ten of the survey respondents who reported high business impact from course participation
- All six of the survey respondents who reported no business impact from course participation
- A random sample of five survey respondents who reported moderate business impact from course participation
- A random sample of eight survey non-respondents with no action plans
- A random sample of five survey non-respondents with action plans

Not all 34 participants were available for interviews. The team was able to interview 23 within the time frame for this project. They discussed the value of delaying the project and trying to schedule interviews with the final 11 participants. Part of the difficulty in scheduling the interviews was that this stage of the evaluation occurred during the height of vacation season. The team made the decision to forego the final 11 interviews because,

- There was adequate representation from each of the stratified subgroups in the slightly smaller sample (23 participants).
- A sample size of 23 participants was a healthy sample size (45% of all class participants); the original plan of 34 interviews was acknowledged to be ambitious and an "over sampling" strategy that was probably not necessary.
- Sufficiently informative data was already obtained from the first 23 interviews.

The group of 23 interviews was made up of 8 "high" impact, 5 "no" impact, 3 randomly selected "moderate" impact, 5 randomly selected survey non-respondents without action plans, and 2 randomly selected survey non-respondents with action plans.

A basic interview protocol structure was agreed on by the team that addressed five areas:

• What was used from the training that worked?

• What short-term or other results were achieved?

• How did these results contribute to business value, such as reduced costs, increased revenues, and so forth?

• What non-training factors helped?

• What suggestions did the interviewee have to improve the program? (optional)

The team listened to Rob Brinkerhoff interview both a high-impact and then a no-impact interviewee. Team members then scheduled time to both conduct the interviews and to type up the notes immediately after each interview. This ensured that the notes were complete and nothing important was forgotten. After the interviews were completed, the team met to review the notes and select the four Success Cases. By discussing the Success Cases as a team, they were able to identify any gaps in the data in their notes. The interviewers noted additional questions that needed to be asked of the four Success Cases chosen and then conducted follow-up interviews to ask those follow-up questions that had been identified and to fill in the missing data in the notes.

Step 5: Communicate Findings, Conclusions, and Recommendations

After the data was gathered, organized, and evaluated, Debbie Kuby and Susan Klieman took the lead in compiling the executive summary and preparing the initial and subsequent presentations to various audiences.

The results and findings were presented to several audiences to accomplish several goals. They were initially presented to the HR Education (HRE) measurement team, the HRE managers, and then the Chief Learning Officer. The purposes of these presentations were to:

- Showcase the ABS program and results,
- Update HRE senior managers on the ABS achievements, and
- Educate the Learning and Development professionals on the Success Case Evaluation Method used to conduct the study.

Next, the evaluation results were presented to the sponsors of the Allstate Business Simulation so that they were aware of the full impact that the program was delivering to the organization.

Next, the presentation was given to the human resources leadership team to:

- Communicate the success stories,
- Market the ABS course for future selection,
- Communicate the cost avoidance and revenue generation impacts, and
- Create an awareness of the SCM methodology with the vice president of human resources and human resource directors, bonus level managers, and human resource business partners.

The recommendations also helped the senior management sponsors and the HR Education course owners fine-tune how participants were selected and how the program was implemented.

The presentation was also given at the Allstate Education Summit, which is a conference for all education employees at Allstate.

Challenges and Constraints

The biggest challenge was time. This project was only one of many that the individuals on the team were responsible for. Trying to get all four team members, the course owner, and the external consultants together for planning, review meetings, and data collection extended the timeline for the evaluation. This was especially challenging in the beginning as the steps in the project were being formulated and input from all members of the team was highly desired. Also, the plan had originally been to have two team members jointly conduct each Success Case interview. This would enable one person to concentrate on asking effective follow-up questions without the burden of having to take extensive notes at the same time. Because the Success Case interview approach was new to the team members and to the organization, joint interviews were viewed as a good quality control process. This proved to be a scheduling challenge and would have potentially caused delays in the completion of the project. Therefore, this luxury was bypassed and the interviewers decided to conduct the interviews with only a single evaluator using a speaker phone.

Although having four people on the evaluation team caused some scheduling delays, one potential scheduling challenge was avoided because there were four team members. By virtue of having four interviewers, it was easier to schedule interview times with participants. There were more options for the participants to choose from, because any of four interviewers could conduct the interview. Also, conducting more than 20 interviews would have taken several weeks to complete, and would have been virtually a full-time job, if there were only one or two interviewers. Having four interviewers allowed the team to schedule more interviews and collect even more data.

In addition to the issue of competing priorities, the team also faced the challenge of finding the right time to survey the participants. Like many large organizations, Allstate frequently surveys employees on a variety of topics. Care was taken to avoid sending out the ABS evaluation survey to the participants at a time when they were being asked to complete other organizational surveys. Finding the right time to send the survey, led to a slight delay, but probably increased the response rate.

Another challenge the evaluation team faced was the uniqueness of the Success Case Methodology. As the team was presenting the process to various stakeholders, some questions were raised regarding the process. These included:

- Why don't we ask more detailed questions in the survey?
- Why don't we ask questions in the survey about specific principles or strategies in the course?
- Why don't we corroborate the examples and data provided by participants by interviewing their managers?
- Why is there no control group?

Responding to these questions and educating colleagues on the process took some additional time. Also, additional interviews were built into the data collection process to satisfy some of the concerns about some participant groups (for example, the group of participants who had completed an action plan, but who did not respond to the survey) that were not included in the original interview sampling plan. However, taking the time to address these concerns up front was actually a valuable process. It increased the perceived validity of the assessment when it was completed and enabled the evaluation team to build in steps to address the concerns.

Results

Of the total 51 participants, 35 returned completed surveys for a response rate of 69%. Of these 35 respondents, 31 of them (89% of the survey respondents) reported some level of business impact (either "High Business Impact" or "Moderate Business Impact" or "Low Business Impact") as a result of the Allstate Business Simulation. Only 4 respondents (11%) reported "No Impact."

In-depth telephone interviews were conducted with a total of 23 randomly selected participants, both survey respondents and non-respondents. Of the course participants, 70% (16 of 23) who were interviewed reported business impact from course participation that could be documented and was considered to be verifiable. 36% of those interviewed confirmed results that were categorized as "high impact" from course participation (8 of 23). Table 13-1 summarizes the nature and extent of business impact verified through the interviews.

Table 13-1 Nature and Extent of Business Impact Confirmed Through SCM Interviews

Business Impact Confirmed by Interviews	Frequency	Percentage of Total Participants Attending Training	Percentage of Interviewed Participants
Total number of individuals who were interviewed	23	45%	100%
Individuals who produced High Business Impact	8	16%	36%
Individuals who produced Moderate Business Impact	4	8%	17%
Individuals who produced Low Business Impact	4	8%	17%
Individuals who produced No Measurable Business Impact	7	14%	30%

If the self-report by participants was 100% accurate and objective, one would expect that the same relative percentages of degree of business impact would appear in both the survey and the follow-up interviews. In other words, if 31% of the survey respondents reported "High Impact," then about 30% of the interviewees would be able to substantiate "High Impact;" and if 34% of the survey respondents reported "Moderate Impact," then about 35% of the interviewees would be able to substantiate

"Moderate Impact;" and this pattern would continue for both the "Low" and "No" Impact groups.

The random sample of interviews confirmed that 8 of 23 interviewees (about one third) were able to produce significant and measurable business impact by applying what they learned in the ABS program back on their jobs. This percentage is relatively consistent with the percentage of survey respondents who claimed "High Impact" (11 of 35 or 31%). This not only confirms the value of the program in helping participants produce measurable and significant business impact; but it also suggests that those participants who are able to produce significant and measurable impact clearly know it.

The rigorous standards applied by the interviewers increased the number of people classified in the "No Measurable Business Impact" category. The percentage of people in this category went from 11% to 30% as a result of the interviews. In other words, although people may have reported (and believed) that the training was helping them produce measurable business impact, an objective auditing by trained evaluators revealed that the degree of business impact was probably being over-stated in the initial survey. The survey showed that only 4 participants or 11% of those who responded to the survey reported "No Impact;" while the interviews revealed that 7 people or 30% of the interviewees were unable to provide solid evidence of measurable business results at the time of the interviews. They may have learned some important information that is helping them in their jobs, but the evidence to date hasn't shown a specific measurable business result.

We also learned that it would have been beneficial to wait to do the evaluation until after the time frame for the action plans was completed, as we interviewed some participants who had not yet completely implemented their action plans. Some had planned to have their action plan fully implemented by the end of 2004 but we did the evaluation survey and interviews in the spring of 2004. While we cannot be certain that these action plans that were taking a longer time would ever really bear fruit, it may have been useful to conduct follow up interviews six to eight months later to determine if some of these "No Business Impact" or "Low Business Impact " participants completed projects and were able to demonstrate measurable results.

The true value of the ABS course emerged from the very valuable outcomes that some participants were able to achieve and that were illustrated in the individual Success Case stories that the evaluation team constructed. These cases illustrate how participants applied principles, strategies, or tools from the ABS to their jobs and the business impact that this had on projects they initiated. As the SCM advises, we would never claim that the learning solution alone was 100% responsible for the achievement of these outcomes. However, in each of the four Success Cases that were presented in the final report, the training was clearly a critical catalyst for success. Critical in the sense that without the training, the managers would not have been able to accomplish the result because they would have lacked:

- The perspective to look at a situation in a new way; or

- The ability or strategy for making the fact-based decisions; or

- The confidence and data to convince senior management of the value of their idea.

From among the Success Cases identified in this evaluation, we included four detailed success profiles in the final report. These four Success Cases were chosen for various reasons, which included:

- A cross representation of learners (different regions, different business units, and so forth)

- Different types of business impact (for example, cost avoidance and revenue generation), and

- The business impact was clearly documented and easily quantified.

Conclusions

As a result of the study, HR Education was able to provide useful information to the rest of the organization, including:

- Evidence that the Allstate Business Simulation was well worth the investment. The study was able to show cost avoidance and revenue generation by the most conservative measures. The Success Cases showed results in a variety of functions and paybacks—for instance, increased revenues, acquisition of new customers, reduced costs, and increased productivity.

- Information on how participants were using the principles, concepts, and skills when back on the job. These cases yielded examples of which course principles were actually being used back on the job right away. This information is being shared with future ABS classes to illustrate the impact the course can have on the business.

- Information on which participants from which functional areas will most easily be able to apply the principles. Although the principles and concepts can be applied within any functional area, it was discovered that participants whose responsibilities involved elements of production had some of the greatest transfer back to the job. This was probably because the computer simulation, which was a significant and powerful element in the training program, had a "production environment" setting. The implication is that more facilitation may be required to ensure that participants from non-production areas are making the links between the principles and their own operations.

- Unanticipated positive benefits resulting from the training. Successes by program participants actually created a "ripple effect" with other employees in the organization. Several participants gave examples during the interviews of how their colleagues initiated process improvement projects in their own areas because they heard about the projects the ABS participants had undertaken as part of the training. For example, one successful participant mentioned that his colleague was implementing a process to save shipping costs on printed forms for the billing department because of work he heard about from the ABS participant's success story.

The Success Case study also identified several key factors in the work environment that contributed to or impeded the participants' ability to obtain maximum value from the course. Some of these key factors included:

- Supportive Leadership: When the course participant's leaders were supportive of the participant, opportunities were taken and implemented back on the job. When the manager support was not evident, other work took priority over the implementation of the course action plan.

- Accountability for action plan or business outcome from course participation: When participants were held accountable for their results, either because the link to the action plan was so intertwined with their job, or because it was part of their Major Responsibilities and Performance Standards, the implementation and success of the action plan became a reality. When participants were not held accountable for their action plan or a business outcome, other priorities took precedence over the implementation and success of it.

- Timing: When course participants had an immediate opportunity or issue to which the course learning could be applied, the training was more likely to be applied.

- Communication of the Selection Process: When the managers selected the participants based on potential use of the course concepts back on the job, the participants had more opportunity to apply concepts learned which resulted in business impact.

In sum, this SCM study enabled the evaluation team to provide recommendations that will:

- Help the organization maximize both the short-term and long-term payoff from the investment,

- Help the participants identify ways and places to apply their new knowledge and skills,

- Prepare the trainees' managers on how to better support the participants in using the knowledge and skills, or even how to nominate the participant who is ready to fully benefit from this intensive development opportunity.

Recommendations

Since the ABS had significant business impact and yielded cost avoidance and revenue generation for the organization, the principal recommendation was that it should be continued. However, the evaluation team made the following recommendations that could significantly strengthen results for future iterations of the program.

- Revise the ABS selection and initial communication process to encourage managers of participants to consider the timing of the course for each participant selected, explain what the course entails so the selected participant has realistic expectations, and explain why he or she was chosen to participate and any expectations they may have of the person.

- Encourage manager engagement before, during, and after the Allstate Business Simulation. Managers of participants should make the course a priority by allowing time for teamwork, should help participants determine appropriate projects for action plans, and should help foster the implementation of the action plan after course completion.

- Incorporate ABS action plan projects into participants' development plans. The accountability in their development plan will help make it a higher priority.

- Incorporate the ABS into the Succession Planning process. Again, the more that the ABS program can be integrated into existing leadership development and selection processes, the greater impact it will have and the less disruptive it will be.

The evaluation team believes that if the organization implemented these recommendations that it would be able to dramatically reduce, if not eliminate altogether, the 30% of the ABS course participants who realized no business impact.

Lessons Learned

In addition to the suggestions and conclusions described throughout this chapter, there were several additional lessons the evaluation team learned in the course of conducting this study:

- The Success Case Method is an excellent, qualitative and quantitative evaluation method. The evaluation team was not familiar with the SCM, but after this experience felt that it provides rich information that can help the organization fine-tune its training initiatives. It can be a useful tool for all HR professionals to do quick measurement of a variety of initiatives (for example, training, marketing, organizational change, and process improvement).

- Participants' stories can be the most powerful evidence of the business impact of training. Trainees from the "high-impact" group have compelling evidence that training does work. In addition to having narrative accounts of their success, including them in the presentation of the final report to senior management is a powerfully persuasive way to convey the hard facts and data.

- Success Case profiles should be included in the final report that illustrate both revenue generation and cost-avoidance. We found that our report had broader appeal and the training was perceived as having more value because we were able to document both types of results.

- Input should be obtained from the finance department to verify the financial results. Their verification of the financial conclusions can add another level of credibility during presentations to the senior teams.

- Know your audience. Be sure you understand what's important to the audience to which you will be presenting the SCM results. Each group will have interest and questions in different areas. For instance, senior managers will be mostly interested in the results and their impact on the business, while Learning and Development professionals will have more interest in the process used in the evaluation. The presentations need to be tailored to reflect those interests. When it comes to presenting the results, the evaluation team learned that "one size" does not fit all!

References

Advantage Performance Group. 2005. "The Advantage Way System." www.advantageperformance.com/businesssolutions/products/Advantage_Way-syst

Brinkerhoff, Robert O. 2003. *The Success Case Method: Find out quickly what's working and what's not.* San Francisco: Berrett Koehler Publishers.

Brinkerhoff, Robert O., and Anne M. Apking. 2001. *High impact learning: Strategies for leveraging business results from training.* New York: Perseus.

Cascio, Wayne F. 1982. *Costing human resources: The financial impact of behavior in organizations.* Boston: Kent.

Gilbert, T.F. 1996. *Human competence: Engineering worthy performance,* ASPI Tribute Edition. Siler Spring, MD, and Amherst, MA: ISPI/HRD Press.

Kirkpatrick, D.L. 1998. *Evaluating training programs,* 2nd ed. San Francisco: Berrett Koehler Publishers.

Mager, R.F., and P. Pipe. 1997. *Analyzing Performance Problems*, 3rd ed. Atlanta, GA: The Center for Effective Performance.

Phillips, J.J. 2003. *Return on investment in training and performance improvement programs.* 2nd ed. Houston: Gulf Publishing.

Tannenbaum, S., and G. Yukl, 1992. Training and development in work organizations. In *Annual Review of Psychology*, 43: 399-441.

Tessmer, Martin, and Rita C. Richey.1997. The role of context in learning and instructional design. In *Educational Technology Research & Development*, 45, no. 2, 85-115.

Rummler, G.A., and Alan P. Brache. 1995. *Improving performance: how to manage the white space on the organization chart.* San Francisco: Jossey-Bass.

Success Case Method Assistance and Resources

Advantage Performance Group, Inc. (APG) is a network of senior training and development experts that has developed in-depth capabilities for supporting impact evaluation in the arena of training and performance improvement. Robert Brinkerhoff has partnered exclusively with APG to provide Success Case Method (SCM) services and products throughout North America and globally. These services include:

- Certification in the Success Case Method in which participants conduct a SCM evaluation of a program in their own organization while receiving scheduled coaching and technical assistance from SCM experts. The certification process enables organizations to complete one or more impact studies while developing internal capability. Certified SCM practitioners and organizations have access to a proprietary web site that holds a growing repository of SCM resources and tools.

- Implementation of impact evaluations where APG experts in the Success Case Method conduct impact studies for a broad range of organizations globally, from government and non-governmental agencies, philanthropic foundations, public schools, to small businesses and Fortune 100 corporations.

- Evaluation consultation, helping organizations plan evaluation methods and strategies, develop internal evaluation capability, structure and staff evaluation units, develop approaches and tools, and so forth.

Contact information for APG is as follows:
Advantage Performance Group
98 Main Street, Suite 336
Tiburon, CA 94920
Phone (800) 494 6646 or (415) 435 3040
www. advantageperformance.com

Index

About the Author

Robert O. Brinkerhoff, an internationally recognized expert in evaluation and training effectiveness, has provided consultation to dozens of major companies and organizations in the United States, South Africa, Russia, Europe, Australia, New Zealand, Singapore, and Saudi Arabia. Dr. Brinkerhoff's clients include leading companies and agencies in virtually all corporate, government agency, and non-profit sectors. An author of numerous books on evaluation and training, Dr. Brinkerhoff, has been a keynote speaker and presenter at hundreds of conferences and institutes worldwide. Many leading corporations and agencies have adopted his methods and tools for training evaluation and effectiveness.

Dr. Brinkerhoff earned a doctorate at the University of Virginia in program evaluation and is currently Professor of Counseling Psychology at Western Michigan University, where he coordinates graduate programs in human resource development. He also serves as principal consultant and CEO for The Learning Alliance in Kalamazoo, Michigan, a firm that provides consultation in training effectiveness and measurement and also offers training and certification in the Success Case Method. He is exclusively aligned and partnered with Advantage Performance Group, Inc.

Dr. Brinkerhoff's work experience includes a five-year stint as an officer in the U.S. Navy during the Vietnam Era, and he also time spent as a framing and cabinet carpenter, a fishing and sailing charter-boat mate in the West Indies, a grocery salesman in Puerto Rico, and a factory laborer in Birmingham, England, where he saw the original Beatles. He has four children, thankfully mostly grown, (at least chronologically) and lives with his wife and several unruly dogs in the rural village of Richland, Michigan. He can be reached at robert.*brinkerhoff@wmich.edu.*

About Berrett-Koehler Publishers

Berrett-Koehler is an independent publisher dedicated to an ambitious mission: Creating a World that Works for All.

We believe that to truly create a better world, action is needed at all levels--individual, organizational, and societal. At the individual level, our publications help people align their lives and work with their deepest values. At the organizational level, our publications promote progressive leadership and management practices, socially responsible approaches to business, and humane and effective organizations. At the societal level, our publications advance social and economic justice, shared prosperity, sustainable development, and new solutions to national and global issues.

We publish groundbreaking books focused on each of these levels. To further advance our commitment to positive change at the societal level, we have recently expanded our line of books in this area and are calling this expanded line "BK Currents."

A major theme of our publications is "Opening Up New Space." They challenge conventional thinking, introduce new points of view, and offer new alternatives for change. Their common quest is changing the underlying beliefs, mindsets, institutions, and structures that keep generating the same cycles of problems, no matter who our leaders are or what improvement programs we adopt.

We strive to practice what we preach--to operate our publishing company in line with the ideas in our books. At the core of our approach is *stewardship*, which we define as a deep sense of responsibility to administer the company for the benefit of all of our "stakeholder" groups: authors, customers, employees, investors, service providers, and the communities and environment around us. We seek to establish a partnering relationship with each stakeholder that is open, equitable, and collaborative.

We are gratified that thousands of readers, authors, and other friends of the company consider themselves to be part of the "BK Community." We hope that you, too, will join our community and connect with us through the ways described on our website at *www.bkconnection.com*.

Be Connected

Visit Our Website

Go to *www.bkconnection.com* to read exclusive previews and excerpts of new books, find detailed information on all Berrett-Koehler titles and authors, browse subject-area libraries of books, and get special discounts.

Subscribe to Our Free E-Newsletter

Be the first to hear about new publications, special discount offers, exclusive articles, news about bestsellers, and more! Get on the list for our free e-newsletter by going to www.bkconnection.com.

Participate in the Discussion

To see what others are saying about our books and post your own thoughts, check out our blogs at www.bkblogs.com.

Get Quantity Discounts

Berrett-Koehler books are available at quantity discounts for orders of ten or more copies. Please call us toll-free at (800) 929-2929 or email us at *bkp.orders@aidcvt.com.*

Host a Reading Group

For tips on how to form and carry on a book reading group in your workplace or community, see our website at www.bkconnection.com.

Join the BK Community

Thousands of readers of our books have become part of the "BK Community" by participating in events featuring our authors, reviewing draft manuscripts of forthcoming books, spreading the word about their favorite books, and supporting our publishing program in other ways. If you would like to join the BK Community, please contact us at *bkcommunity@bkpub.com.*